ROBERT SILVERBERG

Known to thousands of readers for his literary explorations into the past, Robert Silverberg has written *Lost Cities and Vanished Civilizations,* which took readers to Thebes, Carthage, Pompeii, Troy, Babylon, and Knossos; *Sunken History: The Story of Underwater Archaeology,* which was a Junior Literary Guild selection; *Empires in the Dust,* which covered such civilizations as those of the Phoenicians, the Etruscans, the Incas, and the dwellers of the Indus Valley; and *Akhnaten: The Rebel Pharaoh,* about the Egyptian who led his people toward the worship of a single God.

ЛЛЛЛЛЛ

The Long Rampart:

The Story of the Great Wall of China

Other Books by Robert Silverberg:

Treasures Beneath the Sea   Lost Cities and Vanished Civilizations   Sunken History: The Story of Underwater Archaeology   Great Adventures in Archaeology   Empires in the Dust   Akhnaten: The Rebel Pharaoh   The Great Wall of China

ЛГЛГГЛГ

The Long Rampart:

The Story of the Great Wall of China

by Robert Silverberg

Chilton Books

A Division of Chilton Company
Publishers
Philadelphia and New York

Contents

Introduction vii

One: China Before the Wall 1

Two: The First Great Walls 13

Three: Building the Great Wall 25

Four: The Great Wall in Legend 37

Five: The Years of Shih Huang Ti 43

Six: The Fall of Ch'in 53

Seven: The Reign of Emperor Wu 63

Eight: The Troubles of the Han Dynasty 73

Nine: The Barbarians Conquer China 83

Ten: The Rebirth of China 95

Eleven: The Mongol Hordes 107

Twelve: The Ming Dynasty 121

Thirteen: Europe Discovers China 133

Fourteen: The Manchu Conquest 145

Fifteen: The Nineteenth Century and After 159

Introduction

About twenty-two centuries ago, a poet named Antipater drew up a list of the Seven Wonders of the World. Antipater was a Greek who lived in the city of Sidon, then a Phoenician port and now part of the country of Lebanon. His list of Seven Wonders included the most marvelous structures he knew.

Most of the Wonders were in Greece or had been built or designed by Greeks. The only exceptions were the Pyramids of Egypt and the Hanging Gardens of Babylon. The other five Wonders were the statue of Zeus at Olympia, the temple of the goddess Artemis at Ephesus, the Mausoleum, or great tomb, at Halicarnassus, the Colossus of Rhodes, and the Pharos, or lighthouse, of Alexandria.

All of them were truly wonderful. But Antipater left one Wonder off his list, because neither he nor any other Greek had ever heard of it. This Eighth Wonder of the World was brand new. It had been finished in 214 B.C. It was a wall, a snakelike line of stone and brick and mud that stretched for an incredible distance across the northern border of China.

And where was China? You could have gone up and down the length and breadth of Greece, asking the wisest men, and none of them could have told you. Perhaps a few had heard merchants' tales of a land somewhere in the country of the sunrise, east of Egypt, east of Persia, far, far beyond the boundaries of civilization. They might have heard stories of a place where men had yellow skins and slanted eyes, a place that manufactured fine silk robes and other costly treasures.

No man of Greece had ever actually been to that distant, dreamlike sunrise land. So Antipater and his countrymen knew nothing of China's miraculous, wonderful Great Wall. It was not on the list of Wonders of the World. The Greeks of 200 B.C. looked smugly around at their own little corner of the universe. They pointed to a region that ran from Egypt in the East to Rome in the West and said, "This is the known world! This is civilization! All else is outer darkness! All else is barbarism!"

Out in the darkness, the Chinese would have laughed at such proud claims. For their civilization was much older than that of the Greeks. At a time when the Greeks clothed themselves in the rough skins of animals and lived in crude, savage huts, the Chinese already had hundreds of years of art and culture behind them. Now the Greeks talked about the Seven Wonders of the World—but the Chinese had created an Eighth Wonder, the Great Wall.

Why was such a wall wonderful? What was special about the Great Wall of China? Was it made of shimmering marble? Was it inlaid with gold and precious stones? No. It was and is a barrier of ordinary stone, common brick, plain mud. Why, then, was it a Wonder of the World?

The Great Wall is big. It is so big that the mind has trouble imagining its vastness. It is the biggest single structure ever made by man.

How big is big?

The Great Wall of China runs a zigzag course for

some 1,850 miles across China. That's just the *original* Great Wall, the one that was finished in 214 B.C. Later, Chinese rulers tacked 300 miles to the western end of the Wall. Much later, 400 miles were added at the eastern end. There are more than a thousand miles of inner walls. There are some useless loops and spurs where the engineers got lost and built in the wrong direction. All told, the Great Wall of China has been measured at 3,930 miles in length.

Let's forget about the extra loops and zigzags and stick to that original figure of 1,850 miles. Try to imagine what it really means to say that a wall runs such a distance. Suppose we got into a car in Los Angeles and began to drive eastward across the country. We'd pass through the cactus-strewn Mohave Desert and on into Arizona, and in a couple of days we'd be near the Grand Canyon. Then we'd enter Colorado, and our car would make its way over the mighty Rockies. Kansas would be next. Hour after hour, we'd see nothing but endless fields of wheat, ripening in the hot sun. A sign would tell us that we had left Kansas behind and were now in Missouri. At last we would halt in the city of St. Louis, on the banks of the Mississippi River.

From the Pacific to the Mississippi—quite a drive! It's about 1,900 miles: that is, roughly the length of the Great Wall of China.

Pretend, now, that that stupendous Wall ran alongside the road as we made our drive. Not just a line of telephone poles but a massive bulwark, thick and strong, twenty or thirty feet high and fifteen feet wide. Through the baking desert, over the tops of the sky-piercing mountains, across the broad plains, the Great Wall would be our companion for mile after mile after mile.

How big is big? If we put the Great Wall down at the eastern end of the country, it would run from New York to Kansas. If we started it at Rome, it would wriggle across Europe to the shores of Portugal.

The Wall contains enough stone and brick to form a barrier eight feet high and three feet thick right around the world at the equator—25,000 miles. In 1793, when ambassadors from Great Britain visited China, they measured the Wall and declared that it contained more material than all the buildings of their native land. When our astronauts reach the moon a few years from now, the Great Wall of China will probably be the only work of mankind that they will be able to see with their naked eyes.

It is a monster of stone. It lies across China like a gigantic serpent. It sprawls over valleys, up the steep mountainsides, through the thirsty deserts. It dances upon the summits of towering peaks, reaching for the highest pinnacles. It stretches on and on, numbing the eye, a grayish-blue streak, a ribbon in the distance, striking toward the horizon.

The Seven Wonders of the World that Antipater listed have met with harsh fates. The proud statues have long since toppled, the lighthouse of Alexandria lies under the waters of its harbor, the Hanging Gardens of Babylon have crumbled into mud. Of Antipater's Seven Wonders, only Egypt's Pyramids survive at all.

But the Great Wall remains. After twenty-two centuries it still sweeps across thousands of miles of China. What we have today is not the original Great Wall, of course. Over the centuries battalions of men have labored to repair and rebuild the Wall, keeping it strong. Most of the present Great Wall goes back only five hundred years, though it follows the ancient route laid down by the first builders.

One man gave the order for the Wall to be built. He was a Chinese emperor, a strange, cruel, brilliant man.

He wanted to create a boundary to divide civilized China from the territory of the wild men to the north. He gave the word, and all China toiled to raise his barrier. Millions of men slaved to build the Wall. Thousands died. They brought together enough stone to build *thirty* Great Pyramids of Egypt, and they strung a fabulous line of wall across unthinkable distances.

The Great Wall was meant to keep the barbarians out. It didn't. They came through the Wall and over the Wall anyway. In time, they conquered China. Then it was their turn to rebuild the Great Wall, to keep other invaders from doing the same thing. The story of the Great Wall through the ages is one of constant invasion.

Today the Wall is a kind of giant museum piece. It no longer is used for defense. The Chinese have no need for it, because they have better ways of keeping enemies away. There is a different kind of wall around modern China, a wall of words and hatred. The Communist masters of China today fear and distrust other nations. They do not allow many visitors from the outside world. China has become a place of mystery, just as it was hundreds of years ago when no one knew what went on in that far-off, almost legendary land.

The Great Wall can help us, in a way, to understand today's China. Why should a powerful nation want to cut itself off from the rest of the world? Why does China use a great wall of hatred to keep foreigners away? We have to look at the whole story of China for the answer. We have to realize that China has almost always built walls to keep out everybody else.

Let's go back, then, to China's dim past. Let's look at that fantastic Great Wall, that unbelievable serpent of stone, that Eighth Wonder of the World. Let's see who built it, and how—and why.

ЛЛЛЛЛЛ

The Long Rampart:

The Story of the Great Wall of China

One

China
Before
The Wall

The great civilizations of the ancient world all developed around great rivers. Rivers provide water for crops. They allow transportation between cities. They lead people to cooperate to build dams and irrigation channels.

About six thousand years ago, two important civilizations developed in the Near East. One sprang up along the Nile in Egypt. The other arose along the Euphrates River in what is now Iraq. The Sumerians, who lived along the Euphrates, invented a method of writing. So did the Egyptians. They both had systems of government. They were good farmers. They built large cities. By 3000 B.C. both the Egyptians and the Sumerians had rich, complex, extremely interesting civilizations. They were far ahead of the rest of the peoples of the world, who were still backward and primitive.

A little later—say, 2500 B.C.—a third great culture appeared along the Indus River in what is now called Pakistan. These people, too, had vast cities and a system of writing and many other skills.

The next civilization to emerge was that of China.

The roots of Chinese culture go back about four thousand years. Before that, so far as we know, the people of China were nomads, wanderers, who drifted aimlessly from place to place, sometimes building little villages. The homes of these early Chinese were nothing more than holes in the ground. The people learned how to do a little farming and raised scanty crops of millet, a kind of wheat.

About 2000 B.C.—we have no inkling why it happened so suddenly—the Chinese began to gather together in large towns. Within a few generations, they learned new ways of farming and began to raise wheat and rice. They became master carpenters and pottery makers. They invented a way to write by drawing pictures on strips of bamboo. Now there was a fourth great civilization in the world. It, too, developed along a river: the Huang Ho, or Yellow River.

The other civilizations were ancient by that time. The Pyramids of Egypt were more than seven hundred years old. The Sumerians of the Euphrates Valley had already been conquered by invaders. The cities of the Indus Valley were starting to die. But the Chinese grew and flourished while the older cultures were fading away. Today's China can trace its way of life straight back to the settlers along the Yellow River four thousand years ago. No other civilization today is nearly so old. Egypt's greatness ended more than twenty-five hundred years ago. The cities on the Euphrates were deserted ruins by the time of Christ. The Indus civilization disappeared almost forty centuries ago. But Chinese life goes on. It has

2

changed in many ways, of course—but the early foundations can still be seen.

Life along the Yellow River has always been harsh and difficult. The river flows from west to east through the northern part of China, and for much of the way it travels through a plain of unusual yellow soil called *loess.* Loess is a mixture of sand, clay, and limestone. It is good soil for raising crops but troublesome to live on. Loess is soft and fine. A brisk wind easily sweeps it into the air, producing a sandstorm of the sort that the Chinese call a "dry fog." The Yellow River gets its name because it is choked with yellow mud, loess that it has cut free as it flows.

The mud settles in the bed of the Yellow River, causing the water level to rise. Again and again the river has overflowed its banks, bringing death and destruction. This has happened so many times that the Yellow River is nicknamed "China's Sorrow."

The early settlers in the valley of the Yellow River had many problems, then. The loess was fertile, and the river provided the moisture that crops need, so the valley was good farming country. But the river was always a menace. The farmers had to get together to build dikes, in order to prevent floods. One man working alone could not hold back the Yellow River, but thousands of men who cooperated might get somewhere. In that way, the Chinese of four thousand years ago learned to join forces to achieve something useful—the first step toward civilization.

A collection of villages appeared in the valley. The total population may have been a few hundred thousand, at most. The men worked in their fields all day, and the women cooked, sewed, and made pottery. Every few years

3

the river would rise and break through its dikes, flooding the farms and villages. The people would patiently rebuild the dikes and start all over again. Life went on, generation after generation.

Many centuries later, the Chinese invented myths about these early days. They told stories of the earliest rulers. First came the Three August Ones, Fu Hsi, Chu-jung, and Shen-nung. These kings taught the people how to farm, how to cure the sick, how to make silk, how to build large cities.

Then came the Five Sovereigns. The first of these was Huang Ti, the "Yellow Emperor." According to the myths, he "established everywhere the order for the sun, the moon, and the stars." If we can believe the Chinese stories, the Yellow Emperor ruled about 2800 B.C. After him came rulers named Chuan-hu, Kao-Sin, Yao, and Shun. They were wise and kind rulers who did much for the Chinese people.

When Shun was on the throne, the Yellow River overflowed many times. Shun heard of a clever engineer named Yu who had built dams and ditches to stem the floods. "My son has no such talents," Shun declared. "The throne shall descend to the man who saved the people from the flood." Yu came to rule after Shun.

Yu and his descendants ruled China for the next four hundred and fifty years. Such a family of rulers is called a *dynasty*. Chinese historians see Chinese history as a series of dynasties. Just as we speak of an event as happening "when Jefferson was President" or "when Lincoln was President," the Chinese talk about something taking place "during the Han Dynasty" or "during the Sung Dynasty."

The dynasty founded by Yu is known as the *Hsia Dynasty*. According to the old Chinese traditions, it ruled from 1994 to 1523 B.C. There were seventeen Hsia kings

4

in that time. We do not know whether the Hsia Dynasty actually existed, for there is no proof outside Chinese mythology. But probably the cities along the Yellow River at that time were ruled by some family of kings that we can call the Hsia.

The China of the Hsia Dynasty was not the huge China of today. It was still a group of towns in one river valley. During Hsia times, the Chinese began to make tools and weapons out of bronze, started to produce silk, and invented their system of picture writing. They discovered the use of the wheel and built carts and war chariots. Beyond the Hsia territory lived the barbarians—nomads who had no such skills and who lived by hunting and fishing and gathering wild plants.

In 1523 B.C. the stories say, the Hsia kings were overthrown by a new dynasty. Warriors called the Shang came bursting into China, invaded the quiet villages, and made themselves the masters. The Shang Dynasty is not legendary. Archaeologists digging in the ruins of ancient Chinese cities have found relics of the Shang that match the old legendary tales very closely.

The Shang kings were strong rulers. They stretched the boundaries of China along the Yellow River until their territory ran from the shores of the Yellow Sea inland for almost eight hundred miles. They built new cities.

The greatest was their capital, the city of Shang, which rose about 1300 B.C. Shang was surrounded by a high wall made of closely packed earth. It was a splendid and magnificent city. Here the Shang kings held court. When a king died, he was buried with dozens of his slaves, who were put to death so they could serve him in the next world. Into the Shang tombs also went musical instruments, vessels of pottery, war chariots, and even horses to carry the king in the afterlife. The Shang craftsmen were famous for their bronze vases and pots, which were unusual in shape and covered with strange, complex decorations. These bronzes went into the tombs too. All these things have been found by archaeologists. The unearthed relics tell us a great deal about Shang life.

There were about thirty-one Shang kings. In time, they came to rule over about one-fifth of present-day China. But at last they lost their skills of warfare. The Shang warriors grew fat and fond of luxury. In 1027 B.C. they were overthrown by a new dynasty, the Chou.

The Chou came out of western China. They were as tough and as fierce as the Shang themselves had been five hundred years before. They surrounded the palace of the last Shang king and started to break in. He set fire to the palace and died in the flames. The Shang Dynasty died with him. A new family ruled China.

The new rulers divided their land into a number of states. At first there were five states, called Chou, Wei, Yen, Lu, and Ch'i. After a while, more states were added, so that by about 800 B.C. there were fifteen of them.

Each state was ruled by a local chieftain, who had the title of *kung*, or "duke." Each duke had to swear allegiance to the ruler of Chou, whose title was *wang*, or "king." The dukes paid tribute to the king. But the king could not always make the dukes obey him in all things. When the king was a weak man, the dukes of the different states did as they pleased. Sometimes there was war between dukes. Sometimes a rebellious duke even made war against the king.

China expanded greatly under Chou rule. The Yellow River was still the center of the country, but now the civilized region stretched in all directions. In the south, the border was another great river, the Yangtze. In the north, China reached all the way to the bleak desert known as the Gobi. The Yellow Sea was the eastern border; in

6

the west, nomad-infested mountains marked the place where civilization ended. About half of modern China was included in the country. The rest could not be farmed, because it was too hot in the south and too cold and dry in the north, so the Chinese left it to the barbarians.

There was always the danger of enemy attack. A strong state might invade a weak one to carry off slaves and wealth. Or hungry barbarians might swoop down from the north to steal the stored supplies of food. Such raids could come at any time. To protect themselves, the Chinese started to build walls.

In Shang times each important city had been surrounded by a wall of packed earth. Now, under the Chou Dynasty, the walls were made higher around each city. The gates were guarded well and locked at night. Even small villages heaped up ramparts of mud.

Beyond the city walls lay the cultivated fields. The sweating farmers could look up to see the towering walls of the city, where the nobles and merchants and craftsmen lived. When enemy attack came, the peasants left their farms and rushed into the city to take shelter.

The Chou kings tried to keep order. They did what they could to prevent the Chinese states from warring on each other. But the local dukes became too powerful. After a while they hardly paid attention to their faraway king. A Chinese story tells of the downfall of the Chou Dynasty.

It seems that a wise man had declared, "Bows of mulberry wood and quivers of wicker will be the ruin of the Chou Dynasty." King Hsuan of Chou learned of an old couple famous for making mulberry bows and quivers of wicker. He ordered that they be put to death, but a kindly guard let them go, and they fled to the town of Pao, in northwest China.

As they fled, they found a baby girl crying by the

side of the road. She had been abandoned by her real parents. The old couple adopted her and took her with them to Pao. When the baby grew up, she became an amazingly beautiful woman. She was called Ssu of Pao, or Pao Ssu.

In 782 B.C., King Hsuan died, and his son Yu became king. It was the custom for the king to keep a harem of many wives. The loveliest girls of each state were picked to marry the king. The fame of Pao Ssu had spread to the capital, and in 779 she became one of the wives of King Yu.

She was beautiful beyond compare. But she never smiled. Her flawless face always had a scowl or a frown or a look of gloom. King Yu was puzzled. He asked her what amused her. "The sound of tearing silk," she said. So he sent for bales of precious silk and had them ripped to shreds. He brought dancers and jugglers and dwarfs and clowns into the palace. Nothing worked. Pao Ssu did not smile.

"A thousand ounces of gold will be given to anyone who can make Pao Ssu smile," King Yu declared.

His chief minister, greedy for the reward, suggested a way. The royal capital was surrounded by a wall, and along the wall were watchtowers. Whenever barbarians invaded the city, fires were lit in those towers as signals to the dukes of the other states. They were supposed to rush to the aid of their king when they saw the signal fires burning. Why not light the signal fires on a night when there was no attack? the chief minister asked. Then the armies of the states would show up and learn it was all a false alarm. That would be very funny, and Pao Ssu might smile.

The king agreed. Beacons blazed in the watchtowers. In towns nearby, watchmen awakened their masters and told them to get ready to fight. In outlying towns, more

8

signal fires were lit, passing the word to the farthest corners of China.

Toward the capital the legions streamed. Banners flew gaily from the war chariots. Generals in full armor led their troops on. Thousands of soldiers reached the capital, ready to drive away the invaders.

"Go home," King Yu told them. "There is no invasion. It was only a joke."

The dukes were astonished. They had come hundreds of miles for nothing. They gaped at the king, dumfounded. And Pao Ssu began to smile, and then to laugh. Peals of silvery laughter came from her lovely lips. The dukes realized that they were being mocked, and angrily they returned to their homelands.

A little while later, a tribe of barbarians called the Jung went on the warpath. They marched out of the west and laid siege to the Chou capital. King Yu ordered the signal fires lit again. But the dukes remembered how they had been fooled the last time. They did not march again. They left King Yu to fight his own battle.

The barbarians swept through the royal city. They killed King Yu and his courtiers and burned the palaces. The lovely Pao Ssu was kidnaped by a barbarian chief and took her own life. One of King Yu's sons escaped and made his way to the eastern part of China, where he set up a new court at the city of Loyang. The invasion and the defeat of Chou took place in 771 B.C.

After that, the Chou kings had no power except in their own small territory. Each duke went his own way. Some gave themselves the title of *wang*, "king," which till then had only been used by the family of Chou. A new era began, which the Chinese call the Time of the Warring States.

The next five centuries were a period of political

9

confusion in China. We can try to translate it into our own terms by imagining what might happen if a powerful tribe of American Indians were suddenly to invade Washington, D.C., and set fire to the White House. The President and a few members of the Cabinet would manage to escape to Yellowstone National Park, but all of the fifty states would declare their independence, and the governor of each state would start calling himself a president. New York would make war on New Jersey, Illinois invade Indiana, and troops from California would attack Nevada. Before long there would be only eight or ten big states that had swallowed up all the others. One state might be stronger than the rest for a while, but then the other states would get together and defeat it.

Something like that happened in China after 771 B.C. At first there were fifteen states, but before long there were only seven. The state of Ch'i made itself the leading state. Ch'i was in northeastern China. It had a strong army and a well-organized government. From 771 to 636 B.C., Ch'i was the mightiest state of China.

Then the state of Chin came to the fore. Chin lay to the west of Ch'i. Its time of greatest power was from 636 to 453 B.C. The other states around it listened carefully to what the ruler of Chin said and avoided displeasing him. North of Chin was Yen; south of it were Lu, Sung, and the small state of Chou, still ruled by the descendants of the old kings.

Far to the west, a new state was rising, called Ch'in. (There is not much difference in pronunciation between *Chin* and *Ch'in*, but they were separate places, and their names use different characters in Chinese writing.) Ch'in was on the border of the barbarian lands, and its rulers learned much about warfare from the wild horsemen of the north. Two new states had formed also in south-

10

east China, Wu and Yueh. And in the steamy, tropical south, the state of Ch'u emerged.

All these states jostled and bickered and quarreled. Ch'i and Chin and Ch'in fought for the control of the north. In the south, Ch'u gained power over a gigantic district nearly as big in size as all the northern states combined. It was a time of endless war.

It was a time of fear.

It was a time to build walls.

Two

The
First
Great Walls

The many warring states of China had two sets of enemies. One group of enemies were the barbarians, the nomads of the north. The other group consisted of the neighboring Chinese states. Each state had to be ready for an attack by its neighbor and also had to guard against a sudden raid by the tribesmen of the outer districts.

Only one reliable way existed to make a state secure against these enemies, it seemed: to build a wall along the frontier and keep the wall patrolled by armed men. So the warring states began to build huge walls.

The barbarians were always a threat. They had never settled down to become farmers like the Chinese. They raised sheep and cattle instead, living on meat and milk. Since they had to move from place to place all the time to find grass for their herds to graze on, they built no towns or cities. Tents of goatskin served for homes as they wandered.

There were three main zones where the barbarians

lived. In the west was the mountainous, chilly country called Tibet today. Farming was impossible in that frozen desert, and the people raised goats and yaks. In the central region was the great grass-covered plain of Mongolia, also too cold and dry for farming. And in the east was Manchuria, a cold land of forests and rivers. Through these vast territories roamed the nomad barbarians. Life was hard, and they often went hungry. They looked south into China and saw the rich fields of wheat. They could not raise wheat themselves, because their homelands were too cold and dry. So they raided instead.

It must have been a terrifying moment when the lookouts mounted on the walls of the Chinese cities sounded the alarm. Here came the nomads in small bands, a few dozen men at a time. They rode on lean, swift horses and were armed with bows and arrows that they used to deadly effect. Swooping down for a lightning-fast strike at harvest time, they would carry off bags of grain and vanish as quickly as they came. The Chinese armies could do little to stop them; the nomads moved too fast. When troops were sent after them, the horsemen scattered and disappeared in their endless plains.

Building walls seemed like the only defense. For more than a thousand years the Chinese had surrounded their cities with high walls, but those did not protect the wheat ripening in the fields. Now the Chinese started to build walls surrounding entire states.

The records tell us that the state of Ch'i built one wall along its northern frontier in 658 B.C. and another one ten years later. Before long the other states that bordered on barbarian country had walls of their own.

But the barbarians were not the only enemies. The warring states also walled off the boundaries they shared with their Chinese neighbors. This movement grew more active after 453 B.C. In that year, the big state of Chin split into three new states: Chao, Han, and Wei. The political situation became more complicated than ever, and everybody hastily set to work building strong new walls. Thousands of workmen were drafted for this hard labor. In some states, nearly every able-bodied man had to go to work hauling stone and brick to bolster the wall.

So we read in the Chinese annals that in 353 B.C. the state of Wei built a wall to protect itself against its neighbor to the west, the state of Ch'in. Han built a wall on its southern border to keep back the soldiers of powerful Ch'u. Ch'u put up a wall on its northwest boundary to ward off trouble from Ch'in. Ch'i, in the east, ran a wall three hundred miles long on its southern border as a defense against Ch'u. All these states were so busy with their walls that they must have had little time or energy left to make war.

Three states in particular had problems with the nomads. They were Ch'in in the west, Chao in the center, and Yen in the east. They were forced to build northern frontier walls to keep the barbarians back. Eventually, these state walls became part of the Long Rampart itself—the Great Wall of China.

Chao's wall was built by King Wu Ling, who reigned from 325 to 298 B.C. This clever ruler did not simply hide behind his wall. He learned the fighting tricks of the nomads and sent mounted archers into their territory to attack them in their own style.

East of Chao, the state of Yen built a wall for hundreds of miles to keep nomads from descending out of Manchuria. West of Chao was Ch'in, with a wall that followed the path of the Yellow River. By 300 B.C., the general outlines of what soon would be the Great Wall of China were starting to take shape.

One state continued to make war against another. The southern state of Wu was conquered by its neighbor

Yueh in 473, and then Yueh was overwhelmed by Ch'u in 334. Ch'u also swallowed up the state of Lu. Ch'i devoured the state of Sung. But these victories shortly would not matter at all. One of the warring states was growing stronger and stronger and would, in a little while, conquer all the others.

That state was Ch'in. As an ancient Chinese historian wrote, it "ate up its neighbors as a silkworm devours a leaf." Out of the state of Ch'in came the Empire of China—and the Great Wall.

Ch'in was unimportant in the early days of the Chou Dynasty. But after the barbarians burned the Chou capital in 771 B.C., the men of Ch'in saw a chance to gain power and glory. They drove the barbarians out of what had been Chou property and took it for themselves.

After that, Ch'in kept growing until it spread like an octopus over much of northwest China. It had a strategic position, protected on all sides by mountains. As the historian Ssu-ma Ch'ien wrote twenty-one centuries ago, Ch'in's location was so easy to defend that "with twenty thousand men it could hold back a million spearmen." And when the troops of Ch'in came forth to attack the rest of China, he said, "it was like a man emptying a jug of water from the top of a high house."

The other Chinese states were cool toward Ch'in. They did not regard its people as being really civilized. The men of Ch'in were rough and crude. They had mingled too much with barbarians and lacked the polished manners of true Chinese. A chronicler wrote in the fourth century B.C. that "Ch'in has the same customs as the Jung and the Ti," two barbarian tribes. "It has the heart of a tiger or a wolf," he said, calling the upstart state greedy, false, and treacherous.

The many walls of the Chinese states did little to

halt the rise of Ch'in. Ch'in's soldiers were fierce and ruthless. Instead of taking prisoners, as the troops of other states did, they put all captured men to death. Whole towns were wiped out by the flashing iron swords of Ch'in. The other states offered Ch'in bribes to keep the peace. Ch'in took the bribes and attacked anyway.

In 364 B.C., the states of Chao, Wei, and Han joined in a league against Ch'in. They were defeated. In 318 B.C., they united again. This time they were helped by the states of Yen and Ch'i. But Ch'in triumphed and gained more territory. When the big southern state of Ch'u tried to stop Ch'in, it too was defeated.

There was misery in the land. Ch'in had grown until it threatened the existence of the seven other states of that era. In 256 B.C., Ch'in turned against the small state of Chou. Here, the descendants of the old Chou Dynasty still ruled, remembering their long-gone days of glory and grandeur. The King of Ch'in pushed the King of Chou from his throne. The Chou Dynasty was at its end after more than eight hundred years. The other states had left little Chou alone, respecting its ancient traditions. But nothing was sacred to Ch'in.

For a few years after that, the Ch'in advance slowed down. Several kings came and went in brief reigns. With these short-lived rulers in command, Ch'in was not able to launch any full-scale attack on the remaining six states.

Then, in 246 B.C., a thirteen-year-old prince named Cheng became King of Ch'in. A great destiny awaited him. He was the ruler who would unite all China. He would weld the sprawling land into a single empire. And he would build the *Wan-li Ch'ang Ch'eng,* the Wall of Ten Thousand Miles, which is what the Chinese themselves call the Great Wall.

No other ruler in Chinese history would accomplish as much as King Cheng of Ch'in.

No other ruler of Chinese history would be so deeply hated by his own people.

Was he a great emperor, or was he a half-mad tyrant? Perhaps he was both. At any rate, he left his imprint on history. Under his title of Ch'in Shih Huang Ti, he stands at the head of the long procession of China's emperors. To him China owes its Great Wall. Across thousands of miles of Chinese land it runs—the mightiest monument any monarch ever left behind him.

The historian Ssu-ma Ch'ien, who wrote an account of China's past around 100 B.C., gives us this not very complimentary description of Emperor Ch'in Shih Huang Ti:

"High-pointed nose, slit eyes, pigeon breast, wolf voice, tiger heart, stingy, cringing, graceless."

Perhaps he was all these things. Yet he was also a strong leader, a farsighted planner, a bold ruler. It is hard to admire his cruelty, but it is just as hard not to feel awe at his accomplishments.

The boy who was to become China's first emperor was born in 259 B.C. His great-grandfather, King Chao, was then the ruler of the state of Ch'in. King Chao died in 251 B.C. His son, who became king, died a year later. The new king was Tzu-ch'u, Prince Cheng's father. Tzu-ch'u ruled less than four years. When he died in 246 B.C., thirteen-year-old Prince Cheng became King of Ch'in.

While Cheng was a boy, his chief adviser was a rich merchant named Lu Pu-wei. Lu had been a friend of Cheng's father. He was clever and ambitious and seized all the power he could get. But the people of Ch'in hated the scheming minister. In 238 B.C., they rebelled against him. King Cheng, who now was twenty-one years old, put the rebellion down. He sent the greedy Lu Pu-wei into exile and soon found a new adviser, Li Ssu.

Li Ssu was a man from the southern state of Ch'u. Like many politicians of his time, he wandered from state to state, selling his services to the king who would pay most for them. Li Ssu was about thirty-five years old when Cheng became King of Ch'in. He saw that Ch'in was strong enough to conquer all the other states, if it only had the right leadership. "I have heard," he said, "that when one attains the opportune moment one should not be tardy. . . . Therefore, I intend to go westward to give counsel to the King of Ch'in."

When Li Ssu arrived in Ch'in in 246 B.C., Lu Pu-wei was the real ruler. Li Ssu bided his time. He was a shrewd, patient man. After the downfall of Lu Pu-wei in 238, Li Ssu got the ear of the young king. He defeated the attempts of certain enemies at court to have him banished and emerged as King Cheng's favorite adviser.

Li Ssu had a clear idea of how he thought a state should be governed. It was important, he said, to have strict laws, with heavy punishments for all crimes. The people must be made to do the ruler's bidding; otherwise, nothing would be accomplished. A king could not be kindly and gentle. He had to force his subjects to get things done. A philosopher with whom Li Ssu had studied wrote, "If we had to depend upon an arrow being perfectly straight of itself there would be no arrows in a hundred generations. If we had to depend on a piece of wood being perfectly round of itself, there would be no wheels in a thousand generations. . . . How is it, then, that everyone in the world rides carriages and shoots birds? It is the result of applying the art of stretching and bending."

Li Ssu told King Cheng that he would have to apply "the art of stretching and bending" if he wanted his kingdom to be great. He could not let the people relax and do as they pleased. He had to make them work together for the benefit of the state. The best way to do this, Li Ssu said, was to wage war against other states. In a time of war, everyone would do his best to serve the state.

In 235, Li Ssu persuaded King Cheng to renew the war against the rest of China. In the time of the king's great-grandfather, King Chao, Ch'in had seemed about to conquer all of China. But for more than twenty years the armies of Ch'in had remained at home. Now was the time to invade again. "Ours," said Li Ssu, "is such a chance as does not come once in ten thousand years."

A year later, King Cheng sent his troops into battle. First he invaded the neighboring state of Han. The King of Han offered to submit and pledge allegiance to Ch'in. King Cheng did not accept the offer. He knew what had happened to the kings of the Chou Dynasty who had tried to rule that way. He did not intend to let any of the other monarchs of China keep their thrones.

By 230, he had conquered Han completely and occupied it with his troops. In 228 he took the state of Chao, and in 225 Wei. Ch'in now had defeated all three parts of what once had been the powerful state of Chin.

Next, King Cheng invaded Ch'u, the large southern state. Ch'u fell in 223. A year later, it was the turn of Yen, in the far northeast. In 221, the last of the old states, Ch'i, fell before the onrushing chariots of Ch'in.

Ch'in was triumphant in all of China.

It was the first time in five and a half centuries, since the collapse of the Chou rule in 771 B.C., that each Chinese state owed allegiance to the same man. But Ch'in rule was quite different from the loose-reined rule of Chou.

King Cheng would not accept the homage of the defeated kings; they were stripped of their titles and rank. All the noblemen of the conquered states also lost rank and power. King Cheng broke up the old states and divided the country into thirty-six prefectures, or provinces. He named men of his own to rule these prefectures. These local rulers would not be allowed to hand their powers on to their sons. The central authority of the king would be supreme.

Never before in Chinese history had a system like this been established. To mark his accomplishment, King Cheng invented a new name. His title would not be simply *wang*, "king." He would be called *huang ti*, which meant "august sovereign" or "magnificent monarch." He himself would be hailed as *Shih Huang Ti*, the First Emperor, and he intended that his descendants on the throne be known as Second Emperor, Third Emperor, and so on for thousands of generations.

A new dynasty had been founded: the Ch'in Dynasty. China now had an emperor where before it had had many kings. Since the name of the dynasty is placed in Chinese style before the title of the emperor, King Cheng became known formally as Ch'in Shih Huang Ti.

With the wily Li Ssu to guide him, Ch'in Shih Huang Ti proceeded to remake China. He cancelled the laws of the many states and replaced them with a new code of laws good in every part of the land. He ordered that all weights and measures be made standard. Up till then, each state had used its own system. Imagine the confusion if Ohio used a yard that was three inches longer than the yard of Kentucky but five inches shorter than the yard of Pennsylvania! The situation in China had been even more chaotic than that.

Ch'in Shih Huang Ti put one kind of money into circulation everywhere, instead of the many currencies of the old states. He introduced a new system of writing that could be read everywhere in China. He even commanded that the axles of wagons were all to be of the same length. Wagon wheels wear ruts in dirt roads, and the Emperor wanted the ruts to be the same distance apart everywhere, so that one network of roads could serve the whole empire.

With such laws, Ch'in Shih Huang Ti brought order out of the hodgepodge that had gone before. Naturally, many people did not like the new laws. They wanted to go on using their old weights and measures, their old wagons, and their old coinage. The United States had the same sort of difficulties after the Revolutionary War, when the new government tried to create a single nation out of thirteen very different and independent-minded colonies. But this mighty emperor had his way, despite the grumbling. No one dared oppose him.

He built a magnificent palace for himself at the town of Hsien-yang. The swords of the defeated armies were melted down to make twelve huge metal statues, said to have weighed sixty tons apiece, which decorated the palace. Chinese legends claim that the Emperor's palace stretched for seventy miles and was made up of 270 separate buildings. The main building, it is said, was built by the toil of 700,000 prisoners. It had an entrance hall so high that a sixty-foot banner could be unfurled in it. Thousands of people could stand inside the palace at the same time.

But few people actually saw Ch'in Shih Huang Ti. He preferred to be a man of mystery. "I rule without being seen and without making my voice heard," he declared. Towering walls surrounded the royal palace. During the day the Emperor never came forth. Sometimes he rode out at night to inspect his domain, but always in a closed carriage so no subject could see his face.

Hidden away within his vast palace, Ch'in Shih Huang Ti still kept up a fierce interest in the affairs of his empire. From all over China came a steady torrent of reports from local administrators. Ch'in Shih Huang Ti read them all. "He handled one hundred twenty pounds of documents a day," a historian tells us. Of course, the reports were written on bamboo, not on paper, so one hundred twenty pounds of documents would not require Ch'in Shih Huang Ti to do as much reading in his day as the same weight of papers would now.

When he was not busy with problems of government, the Emperor surrounded himself with sorcerers and miracle workers. He wanted them to produce a magic elixir that would allow him to live forever. Men came to him who claimed to be able to enter water without becoming wet, to go through fire without being burned, and to float on clouds in the sky. Each one was allowed to show what he could do. Strange potions were produced and tried out on slaves before they were given to the Emperor. The slaves died, and Ch'in Shih Huang Ti sadly sent magician after magician away, always hoping that the next one to arrive would give him immortality. When he heard that there was a mysterious group of islands eastward across the sea where a "sweet wine-fountain of jade" gushed forth with an elixir of eternal life, Ch'in Shih Huang Ti sent an expedition. The expedition returned, asking that a larger party be sent. But nothing was ever heard from this second group. The Chinese believe that the eastern islands were Japan and that the expedition of Ch'in Shih Huang Ti settled there and were the beginning of the Japanese people.

Another Chinese myth relates the story of a strange voyage made by Ch'in Shih Huang Ti. The Emperor had gone to sleep on a costly rug. In the darkest hour of the night, his soul left his body and traveled to the moon. Looking down on the earth, he saw China, no larger than a dot. "In the midst of the moonshine," the legend goes, "the Emperor took on the idea of building the Great Wall and decided to construct a boundary line for his kingdom, that it might become as one family. The soul of Ch'in Shih Huang Ti traveled from the moon to the earth, took on again its body, and put them to work."

And so the Great Wall of China was built.

Three

Building
The
Great Wall

The real reasons for building the Great Wall of China were less fanciful and more complicated. They were matters of practical politics, not of romantic journeys to the moon.

Ch'in Shih Huang Ti had a problem. It was of such colossal size that it needed a colossal answer. The problem was: how could he hold the empire together now that he had built it? For almost fifteen years from 235 B.C. to the day of victory in 221, he had kept the great machine that was Ch'in running smoothly by turning its strength to war. The war effort had occupied the energies of every citizen. Hundreds of thousands of men had served in Ch'in's army. Those who were too old to fight worked in the fields, cultivating wheat and rice to feed the soldiers. Everyone was busy.

But now the wars were over. All the other states were conquered. No enemies were left. Ch'in Shih Huang Ti controlled a gigantic army with nobody to fight.

He could not simply turn all those men back into civilian life. There would be no work for them to do. They would drift idly about, bored and restless. The Emperor knew that masses of bored men were dangerous. They might serve any master who offered work for them. A revolution could begin, destroying the empire that had just been built. Ch'in Shih Huang Ti had to find a way to harness the seething energy of his idle army.

Fighting new wars was not the answer. There were barbarians in the mountainous south who could be attacked, but that part of China was torrid and tropical, with thick, impassable jungles. It was not a good battleground for the forces of Ch'in Shih Huang Ti. Other barbarians roamed the grassy plains to the north. But they were hard to catch, fast-moving and few in number, and the Emperor did not think it was wise to go after them with his huge, slow army.

No, there were no real enemies available. So Ch'in Shih Huang Ti put his unemployed multitudes to work building a single rampart running more than fifteen hundred miles along the northern boundary of his empire. The old states of Yen, Chao, and Ch'in had each built walls along that line. Now the Emperor decreed that those walls be repaired, extended, and linked to form an incredible barrier, a true Great Wall.

This wall would protect China from the raiding nomads of the north. More important for the purposes of Ch'in Shih Huang Ti, it would keep hordes of idle men from getting into mischief. Probably the Emperor was not worried nearly so much about nomad raids as he was about what his own soldiers might start if they were left with nothing to do.

The nomads were weak and divided at that time. They did not threaten the Chinese very seriously. There were three main tribes. In the east were the Hu, or Tung-hu, occupying what is now Manchuria. In modern-day Mongolia were found the Hsiung-nu. Further to the west were the Yueh-chih, living in what is now Chinese Turkestan and eastern Tibet. The chief differences between these tribes were differences of language. Their way of life was similar. They were herdsmen who drove their cattle from pasture to pasture, pitching their tents in a new place almost every day.

Only the Hsiung-nu were causing any trouble for Ch'in Shih Huang Ti. They had moved down across the Yellow River into an area known as the Ordos. Although they were still north of the old wall of the state of Ch'in, they were occupying land that the Emperor now felt should be included in Chinese dominions. So he decided to drive the Hsiung-nu out and build a new wall north of the Ordos, following the line of the Yellow River.

The Great Wall would have a third purpose, besides keeping back the barbarians and using up the energy of a restless army of unemployed men. It would serve as a line dividing China, a land of farmers, from the land of herdsmen beyond. Not only would the Great Wall keep the nomads out, it would keep the Chinese in!

Ch'in Shih Huang Ti wanted to mark the frontier. "On this side is China, with walled cities and tilled fields," his wall would seem to declare. "On that side is grazing land, where no Chinese citizen belongs." The Emperor knew that the strength of China was in its farms, producing wheat and rice to feed a population of many millions. He did not want his people drifting off into the grassy plains to become nomadic cattle raisers. Ch'in Shih Huang Ti was satisfied with his present conquests. Now he wanted to put up a wall, a band of solid stone and brick and mud that would hold China together. A miser stretches his locked hands out to clutch a heap of gold against his belly. Ch'in Shih Huang Ti wanted to clutch China to him with a Great Wall.

The wall that the Emperor asked for would have to be a miracle of engineering. He was not troubled by the challenge. He had worked a miracle himself by uniting China; now he wanted his builders to perform a miracle for him. He asked for a wall that in many places would be twenty-four feet high and wide enough for eight men to march abreast along its top. Watchtowers every few hundred yards would serve as warning stations from which signals of fire could rise to notify the troops of enemy attack. Bigger towers at greater distances would hold hundreds of soldiers forever on guard against invaders.

Across plain and mountain the Great Wall would go, cutting through soft yellow loess, rising to writhe along the rims of mountains thousands of feet high. At one point, the Wall would be eighty feet below sea level; at another, it would be ten thousand feet above. To build such a miraculous rampart might take years of toil, but Ch'in Shih Huang Ti did not mind that at all. "Let there be a Great Wall," the Emperor declared grandly—and all of China sweated to build one for him.

The actual job of constructing the Wall was given to Meng T'ien. Like Li Ssu and many of the other close advisers of the Emperor, Meng T'ien came from a family of "foreigners"—that is, his ancestors had not lived in the state of Ch'in. They came from the state of Ch'i, in northeastern China.

In the reign of King Chao of Ch'in, great-grandfather of the First Emperor, the grandfather of Meng T'ien left Ch'i to take service in Ch'in. He fought against the states of Han, Chao, and Wei. His son, Meng T'ien's father, led the army that conquered the state of Ch'u in 223.

The third generation of this family of generals included two sons, Meng T'ien and his younger brother, Meng I. In 221 B.C., Meng T'ien defeated Ch'i, his family's ancestral homeland. He and his brother were given high titles by Ch'in Shih Huang Ti. The Emperor treated them with lavish generosity. Soon after the great triumph of Ch'in in 221, the Emperor placed Meng T'ien at the head of some three hundred thousand men and sent him north to build the Great Wall.

It was a task that took him about seven years. He flung up his mighty rampart in broiling summer heat and in winter snow; he led his men up lofty mountains and pressed on through endless plains. Freezing gales, sizzling sandstorms, raging torrents of rain assailed the builders. On and on went the making of bricks, the digging of trenches, the pounding of clay. The old walls were decayed and tumbling down. Some sections of them could be included in the new Great Wall, but in many places Meng T'ien had to build from scratch. Thousands of men died at their toil and were buried on the spot. Thousands more came to replace them. One historian says that four hundred thousand men perished in building what has been called "the longest cemetery in the world."

We know very little about Meng T'ien, the real builder of the Great Wall of China. From Ssu-ma Ch'ien's history, written about a century after the Wall was built, we know that he was a great general and an honorable and patriotic man. But we have no anecdotes that tell us what sort of person he was in everyday life. The Chinese have a legend about Meng T'ien that gives him credit for inventing the writing brush used in the flowing Chinese script. Actually, archaeologists have shown that the writing brush may have been in use in China as early as 1500 B.C.

Perhaps Meng T'ien was simply the man who introduced it to the state of Ch'in, which always was backward in literary matters. It is pleasant to think of General Meng taking time off from building walls and defeating barbarians to invent the writing brush. We can see him seated in his tent at sunset, after a hard day of construction, dipping his brush in ink and covering tablets of bamboo with poetry.

Another mystery is the way the actual building of the Great Wall was carried out. No historian of the time troubled to describe Meng T'ien's methods. We are not even able to depend on the findings of archaeologists. Not much, if any, of Meng T'ien's Great Wall has survived. Its eastern section was rebuilt so many times by later dynasties that we have no idea what it originally looked like. Its western section simply crumbled away from neglect many centuries ago, and what is there now was built within the last thousand years.

But the Chinese are slow to change their ways. We do know how the emperors of a few hundred years ago rebuilt the Great Wall. There is good reason to think that Meng T'ien worked much the same way as they did.

Probably he began by setting up supply bases along the line where the Wall was going to run. These bases—there were thirty-four of them, according to one account—served as regional headquarters for the builders and storage depots for the workers' food. Since there were no farms close to the Great Wall's site, all the food for the workers had to come from hundreds of miles away. The food convoys were slow, and often the food did not 'get to the builders at all. Bandits roamed freely in the newly united empire, and they raided the convoys at will. For example, the district of Shantung sent 182 loads of grain to the workers, but all but one of these vanished before they got to the Great Wall.

After Meng T'ien's supply bases were installed, he began to build his watchtowers, we believe. There may have been as many as 25,000 of them, up to forty feet high and forty feet square at the base, sloping inward to thirty feet square at the top.

The watchtowers were built as close together as possible. Where he could, Meng T'ien put them the distance of two bowshots apart, so that the tower archers could cover all the area around them. The watchtowers were designed to stand out a few feet from the main body of the Wall on the outer side. That enabled the defending soldiers to lean over and pick off attackers below.

Besides these towers, which were intended to be built right into the Wall, there were thousands of others placed north of the Wall as free-standing outposts. These were the lookout towers. They were located on hilltops, on mountain passes, and at the mouths of valleys. Their job was to send advance warning of nomad raiding parties to the main forces along the Wall. Each of these outlying towers was provisioned to hold out for four months in case of siege.

With his towers in place, Meng T'ien commenced the titanic job of linking them with a curtain of wall, stretching nearly two thousand miles.

He used whatever building material was handiest in each district. In the rocky, mountainous country north of what is now Peking, for instance, he built the Wall out of brick and stone. We can suppose that in constructing this section Meng T'ien worked fairly much as did the engineers of the sixteenth century A.D. who rebuilt it.

– Those workmen dug a pair of furrows in the solid rock, about twenty-five feet apart. Along these two lines they piled up foundations of squared blocks of granite, six to twelve feet high and about four feet wide. On top of each of these two bases of granite was laid a brick wall twenty feet high and a couple of feet thick. Between the two outer faces of brick, the builders placed clay or earth, rammed down hard and tight by timber pile drivers or by the stamping feet of many workmen. The last step was to build a brick platform over this inner filling of clay, linking the two brick outer faces of the wall. This provided a roadway along which the defending soldiers could march or ride. -

This method served well enough in the mountainous country. But farther to the west was the loess district, where Chinese civilization was born. There, where the Yellow River makes a big northward loop through the yellow plains, there was no stone for foundations, no clay for bricks. There was only the soft, fine loess. So Meng T'ien's workmen built a wall of loess.

They did it by chopping away at the loess, carving blocks out of it and leaving a ridge standing above the plain. Where the right materials were available, they covered this loess wall with a facing of brick or stone. In other places they put up a wooden framework and filled it with rammed earth. The Great Wall in this district was little more than a heap of hard mud.

Yet it lasted surprisingly well through the centuries. So long as it was rebuilt every few years to repair the damage caused by heavy rains, it served its purpose. An American traveler who visited this section of the Great Wall about 1908 found that, even after years of long neglect, it was still an impressive barrier. In many places it was more than fifteen feet high and fifteen feet thick, with towers thirty feet high. "If mud will do to keep people out," he wrote "why not use it?"

West of the fertile loess region Meng T'ien encountered a barren, forbidding desert. Here, too, he built the Great Wall out of rammed earth. We do not know the exact location of the original Great Wall there, for there are several walls, one within another. Much of the Long Rampart is now covered with desert sand in this section.

Beyond the desert, the terrain became mountainous again. Meng T'ien continued onward, building once more from brick and stone until he reached the frontier outpost of Kiayukuan. There the Wall halted.

There were three main sections, then. In the east, running from the Yellow Sea to the Yellow River's big loop, the Wall was solid and impressive, a ribbon of stone and brick skimming dizzily along the mountaintops. The second section was a rampart of earth, running through the loess country and the desert. Finally, there was the third section, through the mountain country from the town of Liangchow to the western end of the Wall at Kiayukuan.

The whole distance covered was 1,850 miles, including the bends and twists: 800 miles in the first section, 600 miles in the second, and 450 miles in the third. Later, new sections of the Wall were added, more than doubling the original length.

With the Great Wall spanning this huge distance, Ch'in Shih Huang Ti could feel that China was safe against enemies. No attackers could enter from any direction. The eastern boundary was the sea, and in those days there was no danger of naval attack. The southern frontier was marked by thick tropical jungles through which no army could possibly move. On the far west, there rose the mighty mountains of Tibet. And in the north was the Great Wall itself.

The Wall began right at the sea, rising from the edge of the water. Its easternmost point was the city of Shanhaikuan. That name means "Mountain-Sea Barrier" or "Between Mountain and Sea." A high earthen wall, faced with brick and granite blocks, began at the sea and ran three miles to Shanhaikuan, entering the city at a gate called Hsia-tien-ti-e-men, "Under-Heaven-Number-One-Gate" or "The First Gate in the World." A dedication tablet at Shanhaikuan marked the beginning of the Wall with the inscription, "Heaven made the Sea and the Mountains." The Great Wall still begins at Shanhaikuan, but the waves have broken and scattered the blocks of granite at its seaward end.

At the other end of the Wall, Kiayukuan, stands a second dedication tablet. This one is inscribed, "The Martial Barrier of All Under Heaven." Kiayukuan, a city set between rising hills, was the farthest outpost of China. The city's name means "Barrier of the Pleasant Valley." Here all travelers going westward out of China bid a tearful farewell to their homeland as they entered the unknown, unfriendly world outside the Great Wall.

The Wall came to its end five miles southwest of Kiayukuan. The American traveler William Edgar Geil visited the end of the Wall around 1908. He wrote: "During the journey thither no human being crossed our path, and there was not a house in sight the whole way. Five antelopes were the principal sign of life, as they hurried out of our track, and lizards, magpies, and crows, of which there were some to be seen at the start, soon disappeared. There was nothing to attract the eye beyond whirling spirals of sand and tufts of brown sagebrush, while the whole landscape was earth-color, save that on the lofty Southern Mountains there lay, as ever, the snow."

Geil found that the Wall ended with dramatic suddenness at the edge of a steep drop. From the end of the Wall he could look straight down two hundred feet into the waters of the Tapai Ho, or Big White River, which flowed by below.

Beyond Kiayukuan lies the land known to the Chinese as Kou Wai, "Outside the Mouth." They believed it was haunted. Certainly it was a forbidding-looking place. On one side were the sky-piercing fangs of Tibet's mountains; on the other, the lifeless desert wastes of the Gobi. Between the two ran a narrow strip of land dotted with oases. Later, an important caravan route would run along that strip. But in Ch'in Shih Huang Ti's time, the Great Wall marked the end of the known world. No one cared to venture into the howling, demon-ridden wilderness that lay beyond the Barrier of the Pleasant Valley.

Four

The
Great Wall
in Legend

The Chinese are a nation of storytellers. In every village sit wise old men, brimming with the lore of ancient days, who tell tales of China's fabled past. Nothing in Chinese history can set the imagination throbbing like the Great Wall, and the Chinese have had twenty-two centuries to decorate the story of the building of the Wall with fantasy and legend.

And so we are told that Ch'in Shih Huang Ti, the First Emperor, rode horseback across the land, and his horse stamped three times in every *li*, and where he stamped a watchtower sprang up. (There are three *li* to each of our miles.) We read that eighteen suns lit the sky while the Wall was being built, and that the workmen labored so long on it that grass grew in the dust that collected on their heads.

A tale is related of Ch'in Shih Huang Ti's magic whip, which he used to slice off the tops of mountains and to make the Yellow River change its course. We hear, too, that the First Emperor had a magic staff, seven feet long, studded with knobs of iron or gold. The Wall, it is said, was built of any material that was handy, even straw and twigs. When Ch'in Shih Huang Ti struck it with his magic staff, the material was changed to stone.

Even the route of the Wall was laid out by the Emperor's wonderful white horse. The horse wandered freely over mountains and plains, and the Emperor's architects followed it, laying out the line of the Wall along the path the horse took. Once a dust storm came up and the surveyors were unable to find the horse's path. They continued along for ten miles before the dust cleared. Then they discovered that they had gone astray and the horse was elsewhere. The surveyors, architects, and workmen all hurried to get on the right track. But they had already built ten miles of wall going in the wrong direction, which remain today to prove that the story is true!

Near the western end of the Wall is a place where the Long Rampart takes a sharp curve. The Chinese storytellers explain this by saying that while the workmen were resting a dragon appeared and curled up for a nap against a stretch of wall that had just been completed. He was so big that the wall was pushed out of shape. After the dragon went away, the workmen did not dare to straighten it out.

Many of the legends of the Great Wall are love stories. One of them relates how the Emperor lost his magic whip. He fell in love with the daughter of a stone-mason, but she refused to marry him because he was so cruel toward the workmen building the Wall. Ch'in Shih Huang Ti insisted that she become his bride. Instead, she took her own life. Arriving in heaven, she told her sad story to the Dragon King. He was deeply moved by the plight of the suffering workmen and decided to punish the cruel Emperor.

The Dragon King sent his own wife to earth in the form of a marvelously beautiful woman. The Emperor fell in love with her. She teased him into letting her hold his magic whip. The moment she had it, she flew off to heaven with it, and from then on Ch'in Shih Huang Ti had to get along without it.

The story of Meng Chiang Nu is one of the Great Wall legends that has remained alive in China for many centuries. It has been told and retold in dozens of different versions. Meng Chiang Nu was a girl who married Fan San-lang, a brilliant young scholar. Half a month after their wedding, the Emperor began to build the Great Wall, and the frail Fan San-lang was drafted to serve as a workman.

"I am leaving now to work at the Great Wall," he told Meng Chiang Nu sorrowfully. "You must remain behind to wait on our parents." And he set out with the other draftees on the long journey north to the Wall.

Winter came, and there was no news from him. One midnight, the spirit of Fan San-lang came to Meng Chiang Nu in a dream. He entered her bedroom weeping and shivering. "I am freezing to death," he said. "Make me a padded gown. The wicked king has sent me to build the Great Wall, but I have little strength. Since boyhood I have bided over my books. How can I be expected to do this cruel work?"

He told his wondering wife that he had weakened and fallen to the ground to die and had been buried in the Wall. Meng Chiang Nu awakened in fear. She had made warm winter clothes to send to him. Now she set out to take them to him, hoping to find him still alive.

She did not know the distance to the Great Wall. On she trudged through the winter snow for mile after mile, until a merciful goddess took pity on her and whisked her a thousand miles in a moment, setting her down by the Wall. "The width of the wall was several times ten feet," the poem declares. "To east and west you could never see the end of it."

Meng Chiang Nu went among the workmen. "Have you seen the scholar Fan San-lang?" she asked them.

"He is dead," they told her. "He was buried in the Wall."

Meng Chiang Nu began to weep. In heaven, the Jade Emperor looked down and pitied the young widow. He directed spirits to help Meng Chiang Nu find the bones of her husband and give them a proper burial.

There was a deafening clap of thunder. A gaping hole almost a mile long appeared in the newly built Great Wall. The bones of thousands of dead workmen could be seen. They had died while toiling and had been walled up. Which were the bones of Fan San-lang?

Meng Chiang Nu was told how to find out. She bit her finger. Drops of blood ran through the boneyard. Most of the bones were not stained, but the bones of her husband soaked up the blood and stood out, red against the whiteness of the others. Meng Chiang Nu gathered up his remains and set out for home.

Hardly had she begun her sad journey than Ch'in Shih Huang Ti appeared. He "came by that way with officials and soldiers, noble and numberless, with spears, pikes, and swords." Ladies of the court, delicately flickering their fans, rode in carriages. In the middle of the imperial party was a glittering litter, "bright like the sun and moon," upon which sat the Emperor.

He saw Meng Chiang Nu as she passed by him on the road and asked her to stop and tell him where she was going. She related her tale and showed him the bones of her husband. Ch'in Shih Huang Ti asked her to become a lady of his court. If she did not, he said menacingly, she would be put to death for the crime of having caused a section of the Great Wall to be destroyed.

Meng Chiang Nu hated the tyrant who had forced her husband to work himself to death. She did not wish to become one of his wives. But she wanted to live long enough to see that her husband had a decent burial.

"Give me a hundred days to think things over," she begged the Emperor.

He laughed and agreed. "But you must stay with my retinue for that time," he said. "Embroider a gown for me, and then I will let you go home to bury your husband."

Meng Chiang Nu wove an elegant purple-and-gold gown for the Emperor. Ch'in Shih Huang Ti was so impressed by her skill and cleverness that he would not let her go home. He took back his promise and demanded that she join his harem at once. She gave in, but with one condition. "First give my husband a formal state funeral by the shores of the Eastern Sea," she pleaded.

The Emperor granted the wish. The nobles of the court were present, and Ch'in Shih Huang Ti himself took part in the elaborate ceremony. But when the funeral was over, Meng Chiang Nu tricked the Emperor by leaping into the sea. She would not become part of the imperial harem after all. In death, her soul would be reunited with that of her husband.

The Emperor gasped in anger and surprise, "and his face turned yellow." But then he declared:

> To live alone for love is rare in this world.
> There are very few girls like this now to be found.

And he decreed:

> Let a monument of stone be erected on this coast
> In memory of Meng Chiang Nu, who jumped into the sea.
> And now make ready my chariot royal,
> For I will soon return into my court.

Another version of this legend goes on to state that the breach in the Great Wall was never closed and that through all the succeeding centuries the gap remained, until our own time, when the Peking-Kalgan railway line was built through the Wall at that point.

The idea that hundreds of thousands of men were buried in and under the Great Wall is found in many stories. They tell how the workmen, as they dropped, were laid to rest under the growing Wall. One such story is this:

While the Wall was being built, a sorcerer came to Ch'in Shih Huang Ti and told the Emperor that the great project would never be completed unless ten thousand men were buried alive in it. Not even Ch'in Shih Huang Ti was willing to commit such a sinister deed. So he hesitated, and meanwhile the Great Wall remained unfinished.

At last the Emperor found a way of sidestepping the sorcerer's prediction. He sent heralds out through the land in search of a man whose name contained the character *wan*, which means "ten thousand." Such a man was found. He was buried alive in the foundations of the Great Wall.

"I have buried *wan* (ten thousand) alive in the Wall," said Ch'in Shih Huang Ti. And thereafter the work of construction proceeded rapidly.

Five

The Last
Years of
Shih Huang Ti

And so the Great Wall was built across the land from Shanhaikuan to Kiayukuan, a mighty collar shackling China, holding back the barbarians and keeping the Chinese within their proper territory. By 214 B.C., the job was done. Now the Emperor's old problem arose again. How could he keep those hundreds of thousands of men busy? How could he make certain that the restless unemployed soldiers would not rebel against his rule?

He had a troublesome time with some of his advisers, too. Certain men who thought in the old ways came to him and suggested that he follow the pattern of the early rulers. They wanted him to make the local governors of each prefecture able to pass their powers on to their sons. That would create a kind of nobility in the outlying districts. They argued that it was folly to turn away from the practices of the past.

Li Ssu, the Emperor's chief minister, warned Ch'in Shih Huang Ti not to listen. "Times have changed," he said. "Your Majesty has accomplished a great work and has founded a glory which will last ten thousand generations. These stupid ones do not understand this. . . . In ancient days, China was divided up and troubled; there was no one who could unify her. Let us not go back to those dead days," he urged.

He offered a drastic proposal to root out all such out-of-date ideas. "Let all the books in China be rounded up," Li Ssu said. Works of history and philosophy would be burned. That would wipe out "dangerous thoughts" and prevent the use of "the past to discredit the present." The only books that would be spared were those on such subjects as medicine, pharmacy, and farming. Any scholar who tried to keep his books would be punished severely. Only the imperial library itself would be permitted to retain copies of the forbidden volumes.

Printing had not yet been invented in China. The books that existed were written by hand on bamboo tablets, a very slow process. Books were hard to produce, harder to conceal, and easily burned. Most of China's literary and historical classics existed in editions of only a few copies.

The books were collected. The fires burned for days. A thousand years of writing went up in flames. At Li Ssu's advice, Ch'in Shih Huang Ti was trying to erase all of China's past, so that Chinese history would begin with his reign.

Many books were lost forever. Some, hidden by scholars who defied the First Emperor, remained safe. For hundreds of years afterward, supposedly "lost" books kept turning up, concealed in the walls of old houses. Many of the learned men memorized the literary classics and wrote them down again after Ch'in Shih Huang Ti's death.

The Emperor was merciless toward those who opposed him. Chinese tradition holds that 460 scholars were put to death for trying to save books from the fires.

The educated men of China never forgave Ch'in Shih Huang Ti for this act of barbarism. They tagged him with a bitter slogan to stain his name: *"Fen Shu K'en Ju,"* which means, "He burned the books and buried the scholars."

The Burning of the Books took place in 213 B.C. The first Ch'in emperor was at the height of his power. He had overcome the warring states and had unified the land. He had triumphed over the scholars. He had built the magnificent Great Wall, a wonder to endure through the ages.

Li Ssu, though, knew that such glory could not last. He remarked gloomily, "When things have reached their peak, they decline." Ch'in Shih Huang Ti had reached his peak. The decline, when it came, would be sharp and swift.

Ch'in Shih Huang Ti paid no heed to somber predictions. He had an empire to govern. Still looking for ways to keep his soldiers busy, now that the Great Wall was a reality, he sent an army far into the south. The military expedition hacked its way through the sweltering jungles as far as what is now North Vietnam.

Another way to keep men busy was to put them to work building roads. In 212 B.C. Meng T'ien was ordered to build a grand highway across the empire. The tireless general "made cuts through the mountains and filled in the valleys, over a distance of 1,800 li [600 miles]," notes the historian Ssu-ma Ch'ien.

Less than ten years had gone by since the First Emperor had united China. Thanks to his measures, a group of states had become a nation. Ch'in Shih Huang Ti had marked off the boundaries between China and the rest of the world. He had even given the nation the name by which the rest of the world knows it—for most authorities think that *China* is derived from *Ch'in*. (The Chinese themselves, hating the memory of the First Emperor, have never called their own land by that name, though.)

Ch'in Shih Huang Ti had performed wonders. But the people were stirring in dissatisfaction under his rule. He had taxed them heavily to pay for his Wall and his other huge projects. They were weary of toiling for Ch'in Shih Huang Ti. In the outlying provinces, far from the capital, there was talk of rebellion.

The Emperor heard none of it. He remained in his city of Hsien-yang, moving from palace to palace through underground passageways to prevent being seen. He was full of dreams and fantasies now. The magicians at his court held great influence over him. He still longed for the elixir of immortality and took part in strange rites that he thought would bring him long life. He grew vain and boastful and ordered the carving of stone tablets throughout the land that praised his deeds and declared that the Ch'in Dynasty would last ten thousand generations.

The sorcerers were too slow. Time ran out for the First Emperor before they could make him immortal. Death came to him in the winter of his thirty-seventh year of rule and fiftieth year of life. Early in 210 B.C., he left Hsien-yang to go on a tour of inspection of his domain. Accompanied by Meng I, the brother of the wallbuilder, the lonely, aging Emperor traveled, as always, in his closed carriage. He was a thousand miles from his capital when he fell ill and died.

Chaos threatened China. Ch'in Shih Huang Ti had kept the country united through the unique force of his personality. But now he was gone. What would prevent the empire from breaking apart? Who would rule?

The Emperor's eldest son, Fu Su, was the heir to the throne. But he had quarreled with his father about the Burning of the Books. When Fu Su spoke up against that outrage, Ch'in Shih Huang Ti had angrily ordered him to go into the northernmost part of the empire. As the Emperor lay dying, Fu Su and the faithful general Meng T'ien were at the Great Wall, building a new highway.

At the capital city, a struggle for power developed as soon as news of the Emperor's death reached the court. One key figure in the conflict was Li Ssu, the adviser who had helped Ch'in Shih Huang Ti reach greatness. Li Ssu was well past sixty, now, but was still one of the most important men in China. His chief enemy was a sinister individual named Chao Kao, who had the title of Keeper of the Chariots at the imperial court.

Chao Kao was descended from the kings of the ancient state of Chao. But for generations his family had been mean and lowly. Ch'in Shih Huang Ti had been impressed with Chao Kao's shrewdness and raised him to high rank. Chao Kao regarded Li Ssu as his foe, the one man standing between him and great influence.

Chao Kao also hated Meng T'ien and Meng I. Some time in the past, Chao Kao had committed a serious crime. The Emperor had asked Meng I to judge him, and the wallbuilder's brother had sentenced Chao Kao to death. The Emperor then gave Chao Kao a pardon and restored him to his rank, because of his career of valuable service. But Chao Kao was filled with hatred toward the family of Meng.

Now the Emperor was dead, and Chao Kao saw a chance to triumph over the men he despised. He decided to put Hu Hai, a younger son of the Emperor, on the throne. Hu Hai was weak and lazy and greedy. He would do whatever Chao Kao said.

Ch'in Shih Huang Ti had never actually named his successor. But on his deathbed he had ordered that Fu Su come back from his northern exile to take charge of the funeral ceremonies. Evidently the Emperor intended to forgive his eldest son and allow him to have the throne.

Chao Kao saw to it that the message was never sent to Fu Su. The imperial heir remained far away at the Great Wall. Chao Kao sent for the weakling Hu Hai and told him, "If Fu Su returns, he will become established as Sovereign Emperor while you will remain without a foot or an inch of territory." It was easy to get Hu Hai to agree that Fu Su should be cast aside.

Next, Chao Kao visited Li Ssu and spoke cleverly to the old minister. If Fu Su became emperor, Chao Kao said, who would the chief minister be? Not Li Ssu but Meng T'ien! "Your lordship," said Chao Kao, "will not possess for an entire lifetime your seal as Marquis of the Highest Rank, but will someday be returning to your village."

Li Ssu let himseslf be drawn into the conspiracy to make Hu Hai the new emperor. Perhaps he thought that he could dispose of Chao Kao and have great influence over Hu Hai. Certainly he knew that Fu Su would, if he ruled, pay more attention to his good friend Meng T'ien than to anyone else.

A letter was forged, using the seal of the dead Emperor, and was sent to Prince Fu Su at his frontier post near the Great Wall. In it, the Emperor was made to order his son Fu Su to commit suicide, because he "dares to complain and speak ill of all I do." Meng T'ien, "who has not been able to correct my son's fault during this past year," was also commanded to do away with himself.

Meng T'ien was suspicious. He wanted to send a messenger to the capital to find out if the letter were genuine. But Fu Su pointed to the imperial seal. It was

48

his duty to obey, he said, and killed himself. Meng T'ien sent a messenger anyway. Li Ssu took the man prisoner. Puzzled, Meng T'ien set out for the capital himself.

During all this, nobody knew that the Emperor was dead but Chao Kao, Li Ssu, and Hu Hai. They were afraid that, if the news spread before they were in full command, rebellion might break out in the empire. So the closed carriage of Ch'in Shih Huang Ti began the slow journey back to the capital as if the Emperor still lived.

Warm weather had come, though. The imperial body began to decay. To smother the odor, Chao Kao hung a hundred pounds of dried fish on each of the chariots in the procession. No one could tell, as the grand retinue entered Hsien-yang, that a dead man lay in the Emperor's carriage.

Hu Hai became emperor. His title was Erh Shih Huang Ti, the Second August Sovereign. Spoiled and self-indulgent, he left the running of the empire to his ministers. He did not plan to rule with the strength of his father, Ch'in Shih Huang Ti.

Chao Kao moved fast. Over Li Ssu's objections, he had Meng I put to death. Then he put Meng T'ien in prison and ordered him to take poison.

"What crime have I committed?" Meng T'ien asked. He told of his family's three generations of loyal service in Ch'in. Then he answered his own question. "Indeed I have a crime for which to die," he said. "I have made ramparts and ditches over more than ten thousand *li*. I must have cut through the veins of the earth. This is my crime." So saying, he took the poison.

Meng T'ien was serious. In building the Great Wall, he had indeed "cut through the veins of the earth" in many places. According to a Chinese superstition, that

49

was a grave sin. The ancient Chinese belief of *feng shui,* the "science of winds and waters," held that the earth had veins through which cleansing air and streams pass, affecting the pattern of the future. Until very recently in China, no building was done without first consulting an expert on *feng shui* to see if the local spirits of winds and waters would be injured. We may wonder, though, why Meng T'ien did not stop to consider this point until after he had constructed the Great Wall.

With three of his chief enemies—Fu Su and the Meng brothers—dead, Chao Kao now turned to the grand project of building a tomb for the First Emperor. The Chinese tales of Ch'in Shih Huang Ti's tomb claim that it was an astonishing resting place for the mighty monarch.

He had picked the site himself, about twenty miles from his capital. Work had started on the tomb during his lifetime. A great hill of sand had been heaped up. Within it was a palace. The palace contained a huge map of China, modeled in bronze, showing the rivers, mountains, valleys, and plains in three dimensions. The two chief rivers, the Yellow River and the Yangtze, were represented by channels a dozen feet deep, filled with quicksilver. The banks of these rivers were bordered by models of cities and palaces. High overhead was a great polished copper dome on which were outlined the moon and the stars.

The boat-shaped coffin of the First Emperor floated on one of the quicksilver rivers. A powerful bow was mounted on the side of the coffin. If anyone approached it, it would fire an arrow at the intruder. There were stories of hidden trapdoors and secret knives and thunder-making machines to frighten off any tomb robbers. And the tale was told that, when the tomb was sealed, hundreds of slaves and craftsmen were buried alive within it, as companions for the dead Emperor.

Unloved but not forgotten, Ch'in Shih Huang Ti disappeared within his fantastic tomb. The scholars of China never forgave him for burning their books. The ordinary people never forgave him for drafting so many laborers to build the Great Wall. The rich nobles never forgave him for breaking up their power. There were no kind words for the First Emperor.

He had accomplished much, though. He had made a group of states into an empire. He had built the incredible Great Wall, the symbol of China. Tyrant and statesman, mystic and brilliant planner, he was a strange, dynamic, self-willed dictator, a great ruler but a harsh man. The historian Ssu-ma Ch'ien said this of him a hundred years later:

"Ch'in Shih Huang Ti, brandishing his great horse whip, governed the world. He destroyed the nobles and imposed his law on the six directions of space. He handled the whip and the rod to beat the empire. His prestige made the Four Seas tremble. In the south the princes, with bowed heads, handed over their destiny. . . . In the north, the barbarians no longer dared to come down to the south to pasture their horses. . . .

"But he neglected to follow the example of conduct set by the ancient kings. He burned the teachings of the Hundred Schools to make the people stupid. He killed the eminent men. He cherished greedy and base sentiments. He made the foundations of the empire rest on tyranny. If he had governed the realm according to the ways of ancient generations, calamity would not have resulted."

Ch'in Shih Huang Ti had gone his own way, though, little heeding the teachings of the past. And calamity did result, bringing destruction to the dynasty he had founded.

Six

The
Fall
of Ch'in

The year was 210 B.C. The First Emperor was dead. Chao Kao, the Keeper of the Chariots, was in the driver's seat, wielding a furious whip.

"Exterminate the great ministers," he urged his puppet Erh Shih Huang Ti. "Exile your own flesh and blood. Enrich the poor, give honor to the humble, and completely do away with the old ministers of the former emperor."

A reign of terror followed. Twelve of the Second Emperor's brothers were executed, and ten of his sisters, so that no one of royal blood could claim the throne. Ministers of the former reign were killed. In the distant provinces, rebellions sprang up. Ehr Shih Huang Ti did nothing to suppress them.

Li Ssu tried to warn the Second Emperor of the dangers of following Chao Kao's advice. Chao Kao had Li Ssu arrested. After a speedy trial, the old man and his son were put to death. Now no one challenged Chao Kao's power.

Whole provinces broke away from the government in eastern China. The old states were starting to form again, only a few years after the First Emperor had wiped them out. At the capital, Chao Kao concentrated on keeping control of the court, ignoring what was happening far away.

One day Chao Kao caused a deer to be presented to the Second Emperor at the palace. "Is this not a superb horse?" Chao Kao asked.

"Surely this is a deer!" the befuddled Emperor declared.

"It is a horse," replied Chao Kao. "Ask the men of your court if it is a deer or a horse!"

The Emperor turned to his courtiers. Some dared to say that the "horse" was obviously a deer. Chao Kao marked them down as enemies to be dealt with later. Most of the courtiers were smart enough to play Chao Kao's game.

"It is a horse, Your Majesty," they declared. "Clearly it is a horse. Plainly it is a horse."

The Second Emperor thought he was losing his mind. When Chao Kao tried a few similar tricks, Erh Shih Huang Ti retired to an inner palace and refused to see anyone. Chao Kao now dressed some members of the palace guard as "rebels" and had them burst into the palace courtyard to shout and rampage.

Chao Kao himself went to see the Emperor. "Rebels have invaded the palace," he said. "They are coming here to kill you!" In panic, the Second Emperor committed suicide.

Chao Kao took the imperial seal from Erh Shih Huang Ti and fastened it around his waist. He hoped to make himself emperor. But when he came into the throne room, no one would bow to him. He saw that he was going too far by taking the imperial title himself. So he brought forth Tzu-ying, son of Fu Su and grandson of Ch'in Shih Huang Ti, and made him the Third Emperor.

The rebellions in the outer provinces were gathering strength. Chao Kao realized that he could not hold the empire together. In 207 B.C., soon after putting the Third Emperor on the throne, Chao Kao began to make a deal with the rebels. He planned to split the empire, keeping the northwestern region for himself and giving the rest to the rebels. The Third Emperor would be executed.

But the Emperor got wind of the plot. He acted with strength and had Chao Kao assassinated. It was too late to save the dynasty, though. The rebel forces were already marching toward the capital.

A man named Liu Pang was the leader of the revolution. He was forty years old, born to peasants in southern China. He had grown up in "a house where the window was made of the neck of a broken pitcher and where a cord served as a hinge on the door," Ssu-ma Ch'ien wrote in his history of the times.

Liu Pang had joined the army of rebels in 210, after the First Emperor died. He was an honest and well-liked man, as well as a valiant soldier, and he rose swiftly to the highest rank. His army came to the royal capital of Hsien-yang in 206, and he asked the Third Emperor to surrender.

The Emperor yielded. He took off his imperial robes and packed away the imperial seals and insignia. He dressed himself in the rough clothes of a commoner and wrapped a cord around his neck, a sign that he was submitting. Then he rode out of Hsien-yang in a chariot drawn by white horses.

Liu Pang received him politely and took the cord of submission from the Emperor's neck. The Emperor bowed humbly before Liu Pang.

The Ch'in Dynasty was at its end. It was to have lasted ten thousand generations, but it collapsed within fifteen years.

Early in his reign, a sorcerer had warned Ch'in Shih Huang Ti that "the destruction of China will be accomplished through 'Hu.'" The legend goes that the First Emperor took this to mean the northern barbarians, who included a tribe called the Hu. So he built the Great Wall.

But oracles do not always give easily understood prophecies. The destruction of the empire came through "Hu," but the sorcerer was not referring to the barbarian tribe. He meant Hu Hai, the foolish Second Emperor, the puppet weakling who let the great achievements of his father be undone by the scheming Chao Kao.

The old dynasty had fallen, and there was confusion in the land. Another rebel general challenged Liu Pang. A second army arrived at the capital and invaded it. In the confusion, the Third Emperor, who had surrendered to Liu Pang, was taken and killed by the other rebels. The great city itself was set afire. The imperial library, which contained the only existing copies of many classic books, burned to ashes.

It took five years for the civil war to end. Liu Pang was victorious. He became the first emperor of the new Han Dynasty.

His first order was that peace should be restored and all quarrels forgotten. "The troops have not had rest for eight years," he declared. "All the people have suffered severely. Now my efforts in settling the control of the world have been brought to completion." All crimes would be forgiven, he said, except the most serious ones.

Before settling down at his new capital, Liu Pang returned to his native village. He invited all his friends of childhood to a grand party, where he joined them in singing and dancing. The wine passed freely as the old friends of Liu Pang toasted the new emperor.

He proved to be a wise and tolerant ruler. The civil war had left the country in ruins, and people were hungry everywhere. Liu Pang rebuilt the towns and gave food to the hungry. He established the power of the central government once again. In order to get things under control, he made many of his relatives and comrades kings and dukes in the provinces of the empire. It seemed as though he were going back to the old Chou system of having strong local rulers. But once things had settled down, Liu Pang began to whittle away at the powers of these kings and dukes so that the emperor would again be supreme.

Liu Pang had inherited a number of problems from the Ch'in Dynasty. But he had also inherited that dynasty's most important success, the Great Wall of China. And now the Great Wall took on new importance. When Ch'in Shih Huang Ti had had it built, he was more concerned with keeping his subjects out of mischief than in defending his empire against the scattered nomads of the north. Suddenly, though, the nomads were united. A strong leader arose. The barbarians, now that they had an emperor of their own, looked with interest at the wealthy but troubled land south of the Long Rampart. The Great Wall was about to receive its first test as a bulwark against invasion.

The nomad tribe known as the Hsiung-nu had begun to unite during the reign of Ch'in Shih Huang Ti. A chieftain named T'u-man had gained power, taking a title which the Chinese wrote as *shan-yu*, "Great Son of

Heaven." When Meng T'ien's army came north to build the Great Wall, T'u-man decided it would not be wise to do battle with him and led his people northward across the Yellow River. After the fall of the Ch'in Dynasty, though, the Hsiung-nu began to filter back into China.

T'u-man died in 210 B.C., the same year as the First Emperor. An old story claims that he was a victim of the ambitions of his own son, Mao Tun. Mao Tun had command of 10,000 Hsiung-nu horsemen. He trained his men to obey the sound of a "whistling" arrow. He would aim the arrow at a certain target, and all his men had to shoot at the same target. Those who did not were put to death.

The first target of Mao Tun's whistling arrow was his own favorite horse. Those who failed to aim at the animal when Mao Tun did were executed. Next, Mao Tun directed the arrow at one of his favorite wives, and then at a fine horse belonging to T'u-man. In this way he taught his men to aim and shoot at whatever target he picked, without stopping to think.

One day Mao Tun went riding with his father. He drew his bow; the target was T'u-man. No one dared to disobey Mao Tun. The *shan-yu* was pierced by dozens of arrows, so that everyone shared in the guilt of the assassination. Mao Tun took command of the tribe. In short order, he forced the two other important nomad tribes, the Hu and the Yueh-chih, to submit to him.

Suddenly China faced an enemy it had never known before: a strong league of nomads under a single chieftain. Mao Tun was the hero of the north, a superb horseman and a ruthless leader. The Great Wall stood in his way as he planned the invasion of China.

Liu Pang, the new emperor, had his hands full just keeping his own country in order. Now he had to rush to the Great Wall to hold the invaders off. Many of the generals in the northern part of China did not want to fight against Mao Tun. They surrendered quickly to the Hsiung-nu forces and let them come through the Great Wall.

Again and again the nomads erupted into China. The proud span of the Great Wall was almost useless, because Liu Pang could not make his generals remain loyal and defend the gates. But Mao Tun did not wish to conquer China. He had only a few thousand men, and he knew that he could never hope to rule so huge a country as that. He simply wanted to raid the rich land, carrying off its produce to Mongolia.

About 200 B.C. Mao Tun had a perfect chance to overthrow Liu Pang. The Emperor went to the Great Wall himself to fight the Hsiung-nu. But he was trapped in a frontier town and bottled up. Instead of keeping Liu Pang a prisoner in the town, Mao Tun arranged a treaty with him. Liu Pang could go free, but he had to send a royal princess to Mao Tun as a bride, and he had to pay a tribute of grain, wine, and silks.

During the next two hundred years, the Han Dynasty emperors often bribed the Hsiung-nu chieftains in this manner. The annals declare that in 174 B.C. the tribute included "thirty pieces of many-colored woven silk, ten lengths of embroidered silk, several embroidered silk gowns woven with many-colored patterns"; in 51 B.C., "seventy-seven sets of bedcovers"; two years later, "one hundred ten suits of clothes." The Hsiung-nu were sharp bargainers once they found that the Han emperors were willing to buy peace. The northward flow of silk and treasure was immense. Many princesses of the royal blood made the melancholy journey through the gates of the Great Wall, leaving the comforts of China behind to live in the tents of the Hsiung-nu.

So the Great Wall was not proving a very useful

barrier against the enemy. The Wall *could* have kept the nomads out, but the emperors of China were unable to make proper use of it. They could not keep it in repair for all its vast length, and they could not insure the loyalty of the garrisons of soldiers who manned its watchtowers.

The Hsiung-nu kept up the pressure. They raided and were bought off by tribute and raided again. The people of the northern provinces became resigned to sharing the produce of their fields with the nomads. The Great Wall was a mocking failure.

Liu Pang died after ruling just seven years. The Emperor's eldest son was only ten years old. The boy's mother, the Empress Lu, seized power. She ruled savagely, torturing anyone who displeased her. But finally she died and the new ruler brought peace to China. He was Emperor Wen, a son of Liu Pang.

Emperor Wen was disturbed by the raids of the Hsiung-nu. He wanted to do what no one had done in centuries: send an army into the nomads' own territory. But his minister of war warned that it would be unwise to venture past the Great Wall. This is how he described the Hsiung-nu methods of war:

"Scaling and descending the steepest mountains with astonishing rapidity; swimming the deepest rivers and torrents; suffering wind, rain, hunger, and thirst; making forced marches; not being halted even by precipices; accustoming their horses to pass along the narrowest tracks; expert with bow and arrow, and in surprise attacks; discharging their arrows even at full gallop; such are the Hsiung-nu. They attack, retreat, and rally again. If they suffer a setback they simply disappear without trace, like a cloud."

The Great Wall might just as well not have been built. The Hsiung-nu rode deep into China, striking terror in the hearts of the farmers. In 166 B.C. they went as far as the capital city itself before being driven off. Four years later they repeated that feat, and they did it again in 158 B.C. A year afterward, Emperor Wen died. Some said he died of heartbreak and grief because he had been unable to keep the barbarians from raiding his country.

His son ruled for the next sixteen years. He, too, was harried and bedeviled by the Hsiung-nu. He paid the usual bribes and sent a royal princess to the *shan-yu* in 152 B.C. But he could not keep the barbarians on their side of the Great Wall. When he died in 140 B.C., they were as much of a problem to China as ever.

Now there came to the throne a boy of sixteen, Emperor Wu. Destiny had greatness in store for him. The Chinese called him "the warlike emperor." He was to rule for fifty-four years. He would bring the Hsiung-nu to heel, add three hundred miles to the Great Wall, and establish China's first contacts with foreign lands. The reign of the Emperor Wu would be one of the most magnificent in China's long history.

Seven

The Reign of Emperor Wu

It was a time of splendor. The Chinese land was at peace within its borders, enjoying great prosperity. The young Emperor kept the Hsiung-nu at bay. The Great Wall once more served to protect the nation.

Emperor Wu's court was the most glittering China had ever known. Vast and awe-inspiring gardens and hunting preserves surrounded the imperial palace. Two artificial lakes were built for the Emperor's amusement. After trade routes to the west were opened, Emperor Wu had exotic plants and animals brought from distant lands. A court poet wrote of the Empress "gazing about her from the high Orchid Terrace. Amid the perfume of cassia trees, peacocks flocked together, monkeys screamed, kingfishers gathered, and phoenixes flew about."

There was military glory, too. Emperor Wu sent mighty armies against the Hsiung-nu. Some of his expeditions had as many as 100,000 cavalrymen, plus foot soldiers and supply wagons. Often these armies met with frightful defeats in the unfamiliar territory of the nomads. Some were completely annihilated by the speedy Hsiung-nu horsemen. Others were badly whipped and came limping back through the Great Wall with heavy casualties.

By 127 B.C., the generals of Emperor Wu knew a great deal about the art of fighting the nomads. They were able to drive them out of the Ordos region. Six years later, 10,000 cavalrymen struck deep into nomad country and inflicted terrible losses. In 119, the *shan-yu* himself was defeated in battle and had to flee, with Chinese horsemen pounding in pursuit for hundreds of miles. The power of the Hsiung-nu was crippled for many years.

Emperor Wu was glad to take barbarians into his service. When a prince of the Hsiung-nu named Chin Mi-ti was captured and brought to China, he was made a slave at first and was sent to tend horses. But the Emperor noticed him and gave him a position at the court. Chin Mi-ti was trusted by the ruler, and he repaid that trust, for after Emperor Wu's death, many years later, Chin Mi-ti served loyally as guardian for the young new Emperor Chao.

Many of Wu's generals were Hsiung-nu or else were men of the border country who understood nomad ways. Some of these generals changed sides many times, going over to the nomads when the mood took them, then returning to Emperor Wu's banner. There was constant turmoil along the border. Often the Chinese would leave their farms and go through the Great Wall to become nomads; sometimes the nomads would leave Mongolia and settle down in China. The comings and going were endless and confusing.

The Emperor tried to bring order out of the confusion by planting outposts of Chinese civilization north of the Great Wall. In 120 B.C., he sent more than 100,000 settlers to the Ordos. Canals were dug for irrigation, a long wall was built, and farms were established at huge expense. But the land was marshy and unfit for agriculture. Many of the colonists simply drifted away to become nomad shepherds. When the Yellow River overflowed soon after the founding of the colony, thousands of settlers were drowned. Eventually the Chinese withdrew the troops that had patrolled the outer walls of this new settlement, and the Hsiung-nu moved back in.

There were other foreign adventures: an invasion of Manchuria, the conquest of Korea, and war against the tropical southern part of present-day China. But the most spectacular enterprise of Emperor Wu was carried out in the remote west, beyond the end of the Great Wall at Kiayukuan. The Emperor sent an explorer into that unknown region who opened a new world for Han Dynasty China.

No one in recorded Chinese history had ventured into the far west. A legend said that King Mu of the Chou Dynasty had led an army against the barbarians about 1000 B.C. and had gone toward the land of the sunset, encountering no living creatures except four wolves and four stags. Now a young officer named Chang Ch'ien went to follow King Mu's route.

Chang Ch'ien was sent as an ambassador to a tribe of friendly nomads, the Yueh-chih. About 200 B.C. the Hsiung-nu had defeated the Yueh-chih in battle, and they had gone into hiding somewhere in the west. When Emperor Wu came to the throne sixty years later, he wished to have the Yueh-chih return and join with him against the Hsiung-nu.

The explorers set out in 138 B.C. About one hundred men were in Chang Ch'ien's party. To reach the west, they had to travel through the lands of the Hsiung-nu. Hardly had they set foot outside the Great Wall before they were captured and taken before the *shan-yu*. Chang Ch'ien was a captive at the Hsiung-nu court for ten years. They treated him well and even gave him one of their girls as a wife.

Finally Chang Ch'ien escaped. Instead of returning to China after his long captivity, he immediately continued on his mission to the west! Great hardships assailed him as he traveled through the unmapped wilderness. He came to the Ili Valley, where the Yueh-chih were said to be living. But they had migrated onward, and he went farther west, to the city of Ferghana. There he learned that the nomads had turned southwest to a place called Bactria.

The tireless Chang Ch'ien caught up with them there. He tried to persuade them to return to their old territory and join Emperor Wu's war against the Hsiung-nu. But they refused. "Life is good here," they said. "We have no enemies. Why should we go back?"

After a year among the Yueh-chih, Chang Ch'ien gave up and set out for home. On his way back, he was captured again by the Hsiung-nu, but they kept him only a year this time. By 126 B.C. he was back in China. He returned with his Hsiung-nu wife and with a servant named Kan Fu, the only survivor of all the men who had set out with him twelve years before.

He had not managed to negotiate an alliance with the Yueh-chih. What he brought back, instead of a treaty, was a treasure-trove of information about the west. He had brought a whole zoo with him, and a botanical garden, too—samples of the strange plants and animals he had discovered. He brought tales of wealth and luxury, of the rich and powerful territories that lay far beyond the end of the Great Wall. He brought stories of India, where "the country is low, damp, and hot, and the people ride on elephants to fight in battle." He told of Ferghana,

66

where "they have grapevines and many excellent horses. These are blood-sweating horses whose stock is the off-spring of the Heavenly Horses."

Emperor Wu's imagination was stirred by Chang Ch'ien's report. He coveted the "blood-sweating horses" of Ferghana. He yearned for the strange animals of the far-off lands. He longed for the cunning objects made by craftsmen of those distant places. And, shrewdly, he saw that it would strengthen the power of his own em-pire to open contact with the kingdoms in the west.

He launched a full-scale war against the Hsiung-nu. By 119 B.C., as we have seen, the way to the west was clear, for the nomads were driven far back into Mongolia. Soon the ambassadors of Emperor Wu were traveling along what became known as the Old Silk Road, following the line of oases that formed as the waters of melting Tibetan snows ran down to the edge of the Gobi Desert.

Chang Ch'ien himself led one of the first of these embassies, in 115 B.C. He led 300 men as far as the Ili Valley and sent agents onward to Ferghana to obtain some of the famous "blood-sweating horses."

These horses of Ferghana were extraordinary beasts. They were fierce and graceful and majestic, far superior to the stocky mounts of the Hsiung-nu. Emperor Wu hoped to introduce the breed to China, both because the horses were beautiful and because they would be use-ful in war against the horsemen of the north. Chang Ch'ien's agents journeyed to Ferghana with a thousand ounces of gold and a statuette of a horse done in gold as a special gift. But the people of Ferghana would not sell any horses at any price. The Chinese envoys, angry at this, hammered the golden statuette into a lump and strode out. They tried to steal some horses before leaving, but they were caught and put to death.

Several other missions also failed. So Emperor Wu

decided to conquer Ferghana in order to gain possession of the wonderful horses.

A general called Li Kuang-li led an army to Ferghana in 104 B.C., but it was exhausted by the long march and suffered heavy losses. Two years later, Li Kuang-li invaded Ferghana again and laid siege to the city. The city had no wells and depended on a river for its water supply. Li Kuang-li's engineers dammed the river and cut off Ferghana's water. The thirsty city was forced to surrender, and the Chinese captured thousands of horses to take back to Emperor Wu.

The prancing horses of Ferghana, leaping and snorting in the imperial park, inspired Emperor Wu to an even greater interest in the western lands. His ambitions were boundless. Although he had ruled for almost forty years, he was still only in his middle fifties, vigorous and alert. He wanted to make the Old Silk Road absolutely safe for Chinese caravans. The Hsiung-nu, lurking in the desert, were still a threat. Emperor Wu could not wipe them out, so he did the next best thing. He extended the Great Wall of China westward from Kiayukuan.

Emperor Wu's Wall was built for an entirely different purpose from that of Ch'in Shih Huang Ti. The First Emperor had wanted to make use of excess manpower and throw a protective shield across his northern boundary. He saw the Great Wall as something to remain safe behind. But Emperor Wu's Great Wall would help China move outward. The garrisons patrolling the Wall would protect the caravans heading to and from the western lands.

The new section of the Wall was started about 100 B.C. By the time it was finished, several years later, it reached some three hundred miles past Kiayukuan, ending near the city of Tun-huang. Tun-huang was the last town of true China. It was built at an oasis between the mountains of Tibet to the south and the desert of Mongolia to the north. It was heavily fortified, and watchtowers reaching almost seventy miles from the city into the desert gave the defenders early warning in case of trouble from the nomads.

From Tun-huang the two silk roads ran, one going north along the edge of the desert, the other south through the foothills of the mountains of Tibet. The roads met and became one, the Old Silk Road, at Kashgar, more than a thousand miles west of Tun-huang. Then they split once more, heading for the different cities of the west, to Ferghana and Samarkand and the wealthy towns in Bactria and Sogdiana. Finally, the roads led to the kingdom of Parthia in what now is called Iran. The Chinese were impressed by Parthia, which they described as a huge country producing wheat, rice, and grapes, the eggs of "great birds," and wonderfully skillful magicians.

Along the silk roads went camel caravans, winding past snow-topped mountains and parched deserts. Merchants carried spices, furs, silks, and porcelains out of China and returned with wool, linen, glass, precious stones, gold, jade, fine horses, skilled craftsmen, and such exotic foods as raisins. The Parthians were middlemen in this trade. They did business with Rome and Syria, and with China as well. The goods of East and West were exchanged in the market places of Parthia, and Chinese merchants mingled with travelers from Rome.

The new section of the Great Wall was lined with military forts. Soldiers all along its length protected the wealth-laden caravans as they passed by. The Wall was kept in good repair and the Hsiung-nu were steadily forced back. But a time came, about two hundred years after the Emperor Wu, when the Chinese were no longer strong enough to maintain their outposts in the far west. The soldiers were withdrawn, and the barbarians seized the Old Silk Road. The extended section of the Great Wall fell into disrepair.

After a while China seemed to forget that the Wall had ever reached beyond Kiayukuan. Maps of the Wall showed it ending where it had ended in the time of Ch'in Shih Huang Ti. Desert sand engulfed Emperor Wu's part of the Great Wall. Not until the beginning of this century was it rediscovered.

A Hungarian-born archaeologist who had spent much of his life in Great Britain and India found it. He was Mark Aurel Stein, who lived from 1862 to 1943. Stein made several expeditions to the sand-buried cities along the Old Silk Road. In 1907, moving eastward from India to China, Stein passed through the "dreary, salt-encrusted shores" of a dried-up inland sea. He entered a forlorn region that the great Italian traveler Marco Polo had called "the desert of Lop" six hundred years before. Marco had written that the desert was haunted by spirits who would call a man by name, leading him away from his caravan and losing him in the trackless wastes. Stein found no ghosts, but the desert was a dreary, unpleasant place all the same.

One day the dreariness was broken by an exciting discovery: the ruins of an ancient watchtower. It was solidly built and well preserved, fifteen feet square and about twenty-three feet high. The tower was built of hard, well-made bricks of clay mixed with tamarisk branches.

The next day, Stein came to another tower three miles away. He noticed a line of reed bundles cropping out of the gravel soil north of the tower. Glancing along the line of reed bundles, he saw that it stretched perfectly straight toward another tower three miles further on. Stein realized that he was actually standing on the ruins of the westernmost section of the Great Wall of China!

He cleared away the gravel and drift sand and uncovered the Wall. It was fashioned of bundles of reeds, tied and placed across layers of clay mixed with gravel. The bundles were about eight inches thick and eight feet long. The height of the wall, where digging had uncovered it, was about five feet. Alongside it, Stein dug up a tablet of wood inscribed in ancient-looking Chinese characters, so he knew that the ruins were at least a thousand years old and perhaps much older.

He continued on, toward the city of Tun-huang, and followed the line of the Wall for more than fifty miles. In some places it stood almost six feet high; in others it had been ground down by the elements to a height of just inches above the gravel surface. After resting and reprovisioning at Tun-huang, Stein set out again to trace the Wall.

He found another section east of the town and followed it for sixteen miles practically without a break. Here it was eight feet thick and over seven feet high. In the refuse heaps of the watchtowers Stein discovered many slips of wood inscribed with Chinese characters. A number of the slips were dated. "Our excitement was great," Stein wrote, "when my Chinese secretary's decipherment showed that all these dates belonged to the first century A.D. It thus became certain that this ruined border line was occupied already in the Han Dynasty's times, and that I had in my hand the oldest written Chinese documents so far recovered." The documents were military. They concerned records of supplies, troop movements, and the like.

Though sandstorms and harsh winds slowed the work, Stein discovered tower after tower. He knew now that this was Emperor Wu's Great Wall. Each tower had a lookout platform at the top. Here, signals of fire by night and smoke by day could be sent up from tower to tower along the Wall, as had been done in China for thousands of years. The watchtowers had been coated with white plaster that still was intact in some places after twenty centuries. At sunset, the towers glittered brilliantly as the dying light from the west struck their walls.

It seemed to Stein that time had stood still here. "Never did I realize more deeply," he wrote, "how little two thousand years mean where human activity is suspended. . . . How easy it was . . . to imagine that towers and wall were still guarded and that watchful eyes were scanning the deceptive depressions northward for the fleet and artful enemy!" He even found the track in the gravel soil where Chinese soldiers had tramped on their patrols alongside the Great Wall for hundreds of years.

In places, the Wall rose as high as twelve feet. On and on it stretched, with the watchtowers rising in steady regularity even where the Wall itself was worn away. When summer's heat forced him to end his work, Stein returned to Tun-huang. He took with him a large collection of Chinese documents on wood that he had recovered along the line of the Wall. When they were studied, they turned out to bear dates between 100 B.C. and A.D. 75. The evidence indicated that the extension of the Great Wall had been occupied by Chinese troops for about two centuries.

In 1913 and 1914, Mark Aurel Stein followed the line of the ancient Wall for more than two hundred and fifty miles but he found nothing to show that it had been cared for after A.D. 100. Emperor Wu's dream of westward expansion had ended in drifting sand.

Eight

The Troubles of The Han Dynasty

One of Emperor Wu's great dreams was to wipe out the Hsiung-nu entirely, but he never succeeded in eliminating the menace of the nomads. They could retreat indefinitely before his armies, all the way to Siberia if they had to, and there was no way to destroy them.

In 110 B.C., Wu himself led an army of 180,000 horsemen through the Great Wall to attack the barbarians on their own territory. But they slipped into the wastelands and could not be caught. A few years later, another Chinese army that went into Mongolia was surrounded and wiped out by barbarian attackers. Irritated, Emperor Wu put together an even larger force in 99 B.C. under a general named Li Ling. This, too, was cut to tatters by the Hsiung-nu. Li Ling was taken prisoner. He wrote a lamenting letter about his life among the Hsiung-nu:

"All day long I see none but barbarians around me. Skins and felt protect me from wind and rain. With mutton and whey I satisfy my hunger and slake my thirst. Companions with whom to while time away, I have none. The whole country is stiff with black ice. I hear naught but the moaning of the bitter autumn blast, beneath which all vegetation has disappeared. I cannot sleep at night. I turn and listen to the distant sound of Hsiung-nu pipes, to the whinnying of Hsiung-nu steeds. . . ."

Li Ling was forced to remain with the Hsiung-nu for the remaining twenty years of his life. In time the Chinese general was taken into the tribe. He married the daughter of the *shan-yu* and taught the nomads the Chinese methods of war. When Emperor Wu learned that Li Ling was collaborating with the barbarians, he put to death all the members of the general's family who lived in China.

As the Emperor grew old, like Ch'in Shih Huang Ti he spent a fortune on quacks and mystics, searching for the elixir of eternal life. He failed to find it. His great reign came to an end with his death in 87 B.C. His last years had been saddened by rumors of a conspiracy against him, and he had put his eldest son to death wrongfully, thinking he was part of the plot. The throne passed to a younger son who was only seven. But loyal princes, one of them the Hsiung-nu named Chin Mi-ti, protected the boy and ruled well in his name until he was a man.

Instead of fighting the Hsiung-nu, the Chinese began to do business with them. The Great Wall became a gateway for merchants. A Chinese official, writing in 81 B.C., declared, "A piece of Chinese plain silk can be exchanged with the Hsiung-nu for articles worth several pieces of gold. . . . Mules, donkeys, and camels enter the frontier in unbroken lines; horses, dapples and bays, and prancing mounts come into our possession. The furs of sables, marmots, foxes, and badgers, colored rugs and decorated carpets fill the imperial treasury, while jade and auspicious stones, corals, and crystals become national treasures. That

74

is to say, foreign products keep flowing in, while our wealth is not dissipated. National wealth not being dispersed abroad, the people enjoy abundance."

The good times did not last. Weak emperors came to the throne. There were plots and poisonings. Without a strong man at the head of the government, men of powerful families began to assert their independence. Instead of the bold adventures of an Emperor Wu, the times were marked by caution and fear. Few caravans set out for the western lands any more. The Great Wall began to decay and was not repaired.

The only thing that saved China from serious trouble was a split among the Hsiung-nu. They divided into a northern and a southern tribe, each with its own *shan-yu*. The Chinese were friendly toward the southern group of nomads and stirred them up to fight against their northern cousins instead of against China.

There were the usual bribes and tributes. The Chinese sent silks and princesses to the Hsiung-nu to keep them friendly. When Emperor Yuan began to rule in 48 B.C., he decided to send one of his five hundred wives to the *shan-yu* as a gift. But which one should he pick, he wondered? That was easy. He decided to send the ugliest one!

Now it happened that an artist named Mao Yen-shou had been hired to paint portraits of all five hundred wives. Naturally, the women wanted their pictures to be flattering. Mao Yen-shou made them bribe him to paint them with greater beauty than they really had, so Emperor Yuan would notice them. Only one girl, Chao Chun, refused to bribe the artist. So Mao Yen-shou painted her with a twisted, ugly face and added a mole under her right eye. The Emperor, looking over the paintings, found her so bad-looking that he had her removed from his harem.

75

When it came time to pick a princess to send to the Hsiung-nu, Emperor Yuan looked through his collection of portraits again. He decided to part with ugly Chao Chun. The girl was sent for. With five hundred wives in the harem the Emperor had not had time to meet them all in person. He saw Chao Chun for the first time and was startled to see that she did not look at all like her painting —that she was, in fact, more lovely than any of his other wives.

He tried to withdraw the gift. But the ambassadors of the Hsiung-nu held him to it. "You have promised us Chao Chun," they said, "and you must give us Chao Chun." Emperor Yuan offered a camel laden with gold instead, to buy her back, but they would not accept the offer.

And so Chao Chun departed for the court of the *shan-yu*. Her story is a favorite one among Chinese poets. Some of them have written that, rather than go to live in the bleak northern land, Chao Chun hurled herself into the Yellow River where it meets the Great Wall. But in fact she did go to live among the Hsiung-nu and became their queen, with the title of Hu Ning, "The Queen who brings peace to the Hsiung-nu." Many poems tell of her three-month journey across the treeless, wintry plains. In the ninth century A.D., Po Chu-i, one of China's greatest poets, wrote of the hardships of that journey and of the change they must have worked on Chao Chun's beauty:

> Grief and pain and bitter toil have left so deep
> a mark
> That now in the end she is very like what the painter
> made her in his picture.

The lovely princess helped strengthen the friendship between the Chinese and the southern branch of the

Hsiung-nu. Things became so friendly that in 33 B.C. the *shan-yu* actually offered to make himself responsible for the upkeep and defense of the Great Wall! He had come to fear the wild northern Hsiung-nu as much as the Chinese did, and he wanted to be certain that the Great Wall was in good shape in case a time came when his own people had to hide behind it.

The Chinese did not know what to say. It would be easier on the imperial treasury to let the Hsiung-nu pay for repairing the Great Wall. But the idea was too dangerous. Suppose the southern Hsiung-nu became unfriendly again in later years? They would be in command of the fortresses of the Great Wall!

The easy-going Emperor Yuan apparently was willing to let control over the Great Wall pass into nomad hands. But an aged minister argued against it, declaring, "It is now over a century since the Great Wall was rebuilt by Emperor Wu. It is not by any means a mere mud rampart. Up hill and down, it follows the natural configuration of the ground, is honeycombed with secret passages, and bristles with fortified points. Is all this vast labor to be allowed to go to rack and ruin?" There might be rebellions and invasions if the Great Wall were handed over so blithely to the Hsiung-nu, he pointed out.

So Emperor Yuan found a graceful, diplomatic way of saying no to the proposal: "Know then," he told the Hsiung-nu, "that the Great Wall was not built so much to protect the empire against the outer world, as to protect the outer world against the overenterprising Chinese."

Soon after, the Emperor died.

Emperor Yuan's successors were even weaker. By 1 B.C., an adventurer named Wang Mang was able to seize power from the Han Dynasty. Wang Mang was the nephew of Emperor Yuan's chief wife, the Empress Wang. But he was not of the royal family's blood himself, since he was related to the Han emperors only by his aunt's marriage.

For ten years Wang Mang ruled in the name of baby emperors belonging to the true royal family. The last of these children died in A.D. 9 and he made himself Emperor, proclaiming the start of a new dynasty, the Hsin.

Wang Mang was a harsh but energetic ruler. He broke up the large landholdings of the great nobles and gave farms to the peasants. He prohibited the widespread practice of slavery. He imposed new taxes to make the central government strong.

The people disliked Wang Mang and his new laws. They felt he was too strict, and they resented him because he was a usurper. Whenever a ruler finds his own people starting to turn against him, he tries to get their support by starting a foreign war. Wang Mang was no exception. He proceeded to launch a campaign against the Hsiung-nu who had been at peace with China for many years.

He decreed that their territory from now on would be a province of China. He renamed them the *Hsiang-nu,* a jeering name meaning "conquered slaves." And he massed a huge army on the Great Wall frontier.

His tactics only made more enemies for him in China. In A.D. 18 a peasant rebellion, the "Red Eyebrows" movement, sprang up. Thousands of farmers marched on the capital. Wang Mang was forced to use government troops to put them down. That left the frontier army weakened and without reinforcements, so that it became easy prey for the strike-and-run attacks of the Hsiung-nu. The defenders of the Great Wall grew demoralized. Thousands of soldiers deserted to the Hsiung-nu, and the rest began looting and rioting.

Wang Mang drafted one man out of every thirty in China and tried to restore order in the Great Wall provinces. Desperately, he listened to magicians who of-

78

fered to put their black arts at his service. An account written in the following century says that one sorcerer claimed that "he knew how to cross waters without the aid of boats or oars, so that even troops of a hundred or a thousand horses could ride over; another said that it was not necessary to maintain army grain supplies, as he had a medicinal substance which would dispense with food and hunger; a third claimed to be able to fly three hundred miles in one day and suggested that he should be sent to spy on the enemy." Wang Mang tested all these methods but found that they were useless.

Soon members of the overthrown Han Dynasty appeared and began to lead uprisings against the usurper. Liu Hsiu, who was descended from Liu Pang, the first Han emperor, invaded the capital at the head of an army. Wang Mang did not flee. He donned his robes of state and mounted the throne, hoping that no one would dare to strike down the Emperor. He was reciting the ancient writings when a soldier entered the throne room without opposition and beheaded him. It was A.D. 23. The Han Dynasty was back in power. For the next two hundred years it ruled again, and Wang Mang's skull was kept as an ornament in the royal palace.

The new Han Dynasty was not as powerful as it had been one hundred and fifty years before, in the great days of Emperor Wu. Most of the western territory won in Wu's time had been lost through the weakness of later emperors. Independent countries had arisen in the west. Gradually, the Han emperors won back some of what had been lost. The Hsiung-nu were no menace, for they had been hit by droughts and plagues that had killed their livestock and brought famine. Chinese soldiers once again patrolled the Great Wall, keeping the nomads in check.

In A.D. 73, Emperor Ming revived the old dream of

a western empire. Once more, Chinese armies struck westward beyond Kiayukuan to protect the caravan routes along the line of Emperor Wu's addition to the Great Wall. A general named Pan Ch'ao brought the new independent countries of the west under Chinese allegiance without war, simply by showing boldness and determination. For almost thirty years Pan Ch'ao kept order in the west. Chinese influence was felt almost to the borders of Parthia.

If Pan Ch'ao had picked a braver man for the job, he might even have established direct contact between China and Rome. In A.D. 97, he sent a mission to the far-off land the Chinese called Ta-ts'in, or Syria. His envoy, Kan Ying, had instructions to continue on to the even more remote land of Rome, which was little more than a legend to the Chinese.

Kan Ying crossed Parthia and headed toward what is now Iraq. He planned to travel by ship across the Persian Gulf to Syria. There, he could have sailed westward through the Mediterranean Sea to Rome. But while he was still in Parthia, Kan Ying lost his courage. Sailors told him that it might take him as much as two years to sail to Rome, and that the journey would be frightening and dangerous. "He who occupies his business in the great waters is liable to regret and repentance for what he has undertaken," Kan Ying was told. "If the envoy of the Han has no father, no mother, no wife or children to pine after, then let him go to sea—not otherwise." Kan Ying gave the project up and turned back. Otherwise there might have been a Chinese ambassador at the court of the Caesars.

Even so, the western world was learning a great deal about China for the first time. One source of news of China came from Parthia and other countries along the land route west of Kiayukuan. Since this was the Silk Road, the Romans began to refer to China as *Serica,* the land of the *Seres,* or silk merchants. Meanwhile, merchant ships from Egypt and Arabia had found the sea route to China, via the Indian Ocean and the South China Sea. They were doing business with people called the *Sinae,* or *Thinae,* and knew the country as the land of *Thin.* It did not occur to westerners for many centuries that the Seres and the Sinae were one and the same people, that Serica and Thin were one land. The confusion lasted as late as the seventeenth century, as we shall see.

The earliest European reference to China that we know of was set down between A.D. 70 and 90 by a Greek-speaking merchant of Egypt, who wrote an account of a voyage through the Indian Ocean. After mentioning Burma, he declared that the sea ends somewhere in the land of Thin, "and in the interior of that country, quite to the north, there is a very great city called Thinae, from which raw silk and silk thread and silk stuffs are brought overland. . . . It is not easy, however, to get to this Thin, and few and far between are those who come from it."

Few and far between indeed were those who came from the land of Thin, and they became fewer after the retirement of Pan Ch'ao in A.D. 101. The old general, aged seventy, returned to China to die. With his passing, the Chinese lost interest in the western lands again. Soon there began that long sleep of the western Great Wall that was ended only by Aurel Stein's explorations eighteen centuries later.

At home, though, China was having a golden age. It was a period of prosperity, when Chinese civilization made great strides. The Han era was so remarkable for its high state of culture that the Chinese often still call themselves "sons of Han." Science, art, literature, music, and industry all flourished. Astronomers learned how to calculate the frequency of eclipses of the sun and moon. Chinese porcelain making had its beginning.

But darker times were coming. Weak, corrupt emperors took the throne. Public officials became greedy for bribes. There were many assassinations. From A.D. 150 on, the emperors were helpless, and the generals held the real power. These warlords ruled so cruelly that the peasants often rebelled, leading to bloody massacres.

In 190, when a nine-year-old boy became emperor, rival generals attacked the capital. It was burned and pillaged. The government records were destroyed, and the tombs of the Han emperors were looted. The country began to split apart. Three warlords, Ts'ao Ts'ao in the north, Liu Pei in the west, and Sun Ts'e in the east, seized control. By A.D. 220 the last Han emperor had been pushed from his shaky throne. China split into three separate kingdoms and entered a time of trouble that before long would see barbarians from the north in command of the country.

Nine

The
Barbarians
Conquer China

China had gone back to the conditions of the Time of the Warring States. The great achievement of Ch'in Shih Huang Ti had been undone. Out of the once-unified empire came the splinter kingdoms of Wei, Shu, and Wu.

Wei was the northern and western part of China, running to the Great Wall. Wu was the hot, forested, rice-growing region of the Yangtze Valley. Shu was the southwestern district now known as Szechuan.

The three kingdoms warred on one another. In 264, Wei conquered Shu. In 280, Wu also fell, and China was once again united. The new dynasty took the name of Chin. Its most important ruler was Emperor Wu, called Chin Wu to distinguish him from the great Emperor Wu of the Han Dynasty.

Chin Wu was never in a really strong position; the nomads were on the warpath once again. The Hsiung-nu no longer threatened China. Most of them had migrated toward the west, where known as the Huns, they invaded Europe and brought terror to the Roman Empire. But there were new barbarian tribes, the Hsien-pi and their relatives the T'o-pa, who were growing uncomfortably powerful. Emperor Chin Wu met the challenge in a traditional way: he rebuilt the Great Wall.

In so doing, he ignored the counsel of one of his own advisers, a man named Chang Tsai. In 280, Chang Tsai had won fame for an inscription he wrote on a mountain wall, calling upon the people to "trust in virtue, not in walls." Chin Wu preferred to trust in walls. Much of the western section of the Great Wall had tumbled apart during the troubled time of the three kingdoms, and the Emperor had it repaired, with new watchtowers added.

It was too late to stop the barbarians. They had come drifting through the Great Wall over the past sixty or seventy years, taking control of the northern provinces. Chin Wu could not drive them out. He had to buy their allegiance by offering them titles and tribute. By the year 300, the nomads were masters of the districts just south of the Great Wall. China's miraculous northern barrier no longer gave any protection.

The Emperor made a fatal mistake. He invited a tribe of Huns to drive out the other tribes of nomad raiders. It was a case of "bringing in lions to help get rid of dogs." The Huns grabbed the northern provinces from the other barbarians and moved steadily southward. By 311, they were deep into the territory of the Chin Dynasty. They captured the capital and, in 316, took the Emperor himself prisoner and executed him.

The surviving members of the Chin Dynasty family fled to the southeast and set up a capital at the city of Nanking. The Chin Dynasty managed to survive there for more than a century, from 317 to 419. But the whole northern half of China was in barbarian hands.

Now tribe after tribe of nomads scampered through the passes of the Great Wall, and dynasty after barbarian dynasty held sway along the frontier. During the next hundred years there were no less than eighteen dynasties, some of them ruling at the same time as others. China north of the Chin domain split into many tiny states, each with its own ruling dynasty. Most of these rulers were foreign barbarians—some Tibetans, some Huns, some Hsien-pi.

A curious thing occurred: the barbarians turned into Chinese themselves. Again and again, some tribe of northern warriors would pitch tents south of the Great Wall as conquerors and then begin to adopt Chinese names and Chinese customs. They would slip by easy stages into becoming Chinese in every way, leaving themselves open to the attack of tougher, more barbaric invaders. Each wave of invaders in turn went through the same process.

During the confusion of the late fourth century, new conquerors appeared who swept through the Great Wall, tumbled the petty emperors into oblivion, and set up a new and lasting dynasty. They were the T'o-pa, a branch of the Hsien-pi. At first they came in small numbers, slipping through the Great Wall and adopting Chinese names, customs, and dress. About 385, there were so many of them that they began to grow powerful. They attacked and defeated one small state after another. By 398, the T'o-pa ruler proclaimed himself emperor of the Wei Dynasty. Within forty years, the T'o-pa ruled all of northern China.

The Wei Dynasty rulers were more intelligent in their approach to governing China than the other nomads had been. The others, finding themselves masters of a population consisting of millions of farmers, had tried to turn everybody into shepherds. But the Chinese did not know how to live in nomad fashion. Starvation struck as the farms went out of production, and the great famines helped to overthrow the barbarian masters.

The T'o-pa emperors did not try to make nomads out of the Chinese. They staffed their government with Chinese officials and kept everything in China as it always had been, with themselves in charge. They adopted Chinese as their own language. They let Chinese men marry T'o-pa women. They gave themselves Chinese family names.

So Chinese did the T'o-pa become, in fact, that they began repairing the Great Wall to fend off their barbarian relatives of the north! In 423, Emperor T'o-pa Ssu built a six-hundred-mile section of new wall following the original line of Ch'in Shih Huang Ti. It was meant to hold back the raiding parties of a new nomad tribe, the Juan-juan.

The next Wei Dynasty ruler, T'o-pa Tao, continued his father's work of repairing the Great Wall during his sixteen-year rule. He even added a completely new section. It ran from east to west through Kalgan, an important marketing town north of Peking. Stretching for four hundred miles, this new wall lay seventy miles north of Ch'in Shih Huang Ti's Great Wall, which now became an inner line of defense. T'o-pa Tao also built a long rampart of tamped earth from north to south on his western frontier to keep away a rampaging Hun tribe called the Hsia.

There is something a little comical about this. Only three generations away from nomad life himself, T'o-pa Tao had taken the responsibility of shielding his adopted country from the onslaught of the wild men of the north. But he did not forget barbarian ways of making war. He sent fast-paced cavalry troops beyond the Great Wall to swoop down on the Juan-juan and other enemies. By 429, the Juan-juan no longer threatened the wheat fields of China.

T'o-pa Tao also tried to conquer southern China. In this he had no luck. The native-born rulers of the south kept the T'o-pa armies stalemated for thirty years, and the war was called off. But in the far west the T'o-pa were more successful. They defeated the many small states that had sprung up there. Now they controlled all of north China. It became possible to reopen trade with the west. Caravans once again traveled the Old Silk Road and Chinese merchants were seen as far away as India.

Some religious pilgrims went that way also, for Buddhism had taken hold in China now, and there were many who wished to visit the Buddhist shrines in India. Buddhism had been founded about 500 B.C. The peaceful religion had spread slowly eastward, and it began to grow popular in China about A.D. 300. The T'o-pa encouraged the new religion, saying, "Buddha, being a barbarian god, is the one we should worship."

The Chinese pilgrims traveled as much as 10,000 miles on their journeys to India and back, much of it on foot. One of the most famous pilgrims was Fa-hsien, who passed through the western frontier town of Tun-huang in 399. He wrote, "The Governor of Tun-huang, by name Li Hao, gave us all necessaries for crossing the desert of Gobi. In this desert there are a great many evil spirits and also hot winds; those who encounter them perish to a man. There are neither birds above nor beasts below. Gazing on all sides as far as the eye can reach in order to mark the track, no guidance is to be obtained save from the rotting bones of dead men, which point the way."

The last watchtowers of the Great Wall vanished in the east. Fa-hsien and the other pilgrims made their way across the haunted desert to the city of Khotan, and from there to India. The trip took him six years. He spent six more years studying at the Buddhist temple there. Fa-hsien returned to China in 414 and wrote a famous account of his long pilgrimage.

With caravans going to and fro, the T'o-pa emperors developed a great love of luxury. They grew soft and lazy. They moved their capital from a cold, stormswept city in the north to a kinder climate far from the Great Wall. They continued to try to conquer the southern half of China, still under the rule of true Chinese. But they failed, and the effort made them even weaker.

The T'o-pa who lived near the Great Wall felt nothing but contempt for their relatives at the royal court. These northerners were still fierce tribesmen, and they revolted against the easy-going Wei Dynasty. The upheaval that followed destroyed the power of the T'o-pa rulers. After a century and a half of control, they were overthrown about 550. They had been strong leaders at first, but the lure of Chinese culture had been fatal to them. Giving up warfare and horsemanship for wine and poetry, the T'o-pa had grown soft and were swallowed up by their enemies.

Now many dynasties ruled at once. In the northwest, a murderous, barbaric crew of Hsien-pi nomads founded the Northern Chou Dynasty. In the northeast, the Chinese themselves gained control and proclaimed the Northern Ch'i Dynasty. The Northern Ch'i immediately showed their Chinese nature by building long walls.

They started by strengthening the wall that had been built by the T'o-pa in the west, running from north to south. Then they began building a new wall three hundred miles long, following the original line of the Great Wall. The records say that 1,800,000 men worked on this project, beginning in A.D. 555. Maybe that was an exaggeration—but the work was done well, because it was still in good shape nine hundred years later when another dynasty reconstructed that part of the Great Wall. Some sections of the wall built by the Northern Ch'i are probably still in existence and are the oldest surviving parts of the eastern Great Wall.

While these two dynasties fought in the north, everything was in confusion in the south. Dynasties came quickly to power and fell as quickly, like blinking fireflies. For a few years, a T'o-pa general named Hou Ching made himself Emperor. That was the first time a northern barbarian had ever held the throne of southern China. But he was soon overthrown.

North of the Great Wall a new nomad empire was taking shape. A tribe that had been subject to the Juan-juan rebelled and drove the former masters right out of Asia. The Chinese called the rebels the T'u-chueh. The Juan-juan spoke of them as the Turkut. They were the ancestors of the people we call the Turks.

The T'u-chueh, once they had driven out the Juan-juan, put together a vast domain within fifteen years. By about 560, they ruled all of northern Asia, from Mongolia to Afghanistan. Ambassadors of the T'u-chueh appeared at the courts of such great powers as Byzantium and Persia. They arrived at the capital city of the Northern Chou Dynasty, too. The Northern Chou Emperor was as gracious and polite as he knew how to be, when these Turkish envoys came swaggering into his realm.

The T'u-chueh and the Northern Chou joined forces and destroyed the Northern Ch'i Dynasty. Now all of northern China was under one rule again. But the Northern Chou Emperor was only a puppet of the powerful T'u-chueh. It seemed just a matter of time before the barbarians would push him aside and add China to their mushrooming empire. But that did not happen. Some unexpected events gave China back to the Chinese.

In 580, the Northern Chou Emperor, Hsuan, died. A boy came to the throne, but he was not destined to rule for long. The chief minister of the land was a Chinese man named Yang Chien, who had been the real ruler for several years. Seeing his chance, Yang Chien slew the boy Emperor in 581, along with fifty-nine royal princes. He named himself as the first emperor of the Sui Dynasty.

The T'u-chueh could do nothing to halt the rise of this strong new monarch. They had troubles of their own. Their huge empire, put together too rapidly, broke in half. There was civil war between the eastern Turks and the western Turks. Before they could recover from their split, Yang Chien had an unbreakable grip on China.

He established a strong central government. By 585 he was master of the entire north. Now Yang Chien looked toward the Turks. They were becoming dangerous again. He fortified the frontier and lost no time in strengthening the Great Wall.

For the sixth time since the days of Emperor Wu, seven hundred years before, the Wall received a full-scale reconstruction. Yang Chien also had it extended. His addition to the Great Wall cut diagonally across the loop of the Yellow River, leaving the Ordos mostly to the Turks. The new wall ran some two hundred miles west of the river, and 30,000 men were assigned to the task of its construction. For the rest of Yang Chien's reign there was never-ending repair work on the Great Wall.

With the control of the north secure, Yang Chien marched south in 587. By 589, he had conquered it all. He ruled over much the same vast empire that had first been put together by Ch'in Shih Huang Ti.

Shrewdly, he kept the eastern and western Turkish factions at odds with each other. Through a series of complicated alliances, Yang Chien divided the Turks into still smaller parties and reduced their power.

He had trouble within his own family. Yang Chien

quarreled with his eldest son, the heir to the throne, and set him aside in favor of Kuang, a younger son. Kuang immediately murdered his brother to keep him from returning to favor. In 604, Yang Chien himself died, quite suddenly. Possibly he was also a victim of Kuang's ambitions. One story says that the prince was seen thrusting a dagger into the heart of a clay image on which Yang Chien's name had been written—using magic to murder his father. Other tales hint darkly of poison.

The new emperor styled himself Yang Ti. He was like Ch'in Shih Huang Ti in many ways. He lived in great splendor and made China work hard to build awesome projects. For his own pleasure, he founded a new capital city at Yangchow, in the south, although he had two other capitals in the north that a more modest ruler might have found satisfactory. At one of the northern capitals, Loyang, Yang Ti constructed an immense palace on the shores of an artificial lake. Sixteen villas for his sixteen favorite wives lined the banks of the river that fed the artificial lake. A park some seventy miles around surrounded the entire imperial area.

Along the road from Loyang to the other northern capital, Ch'ang-an, Yang Ti erected forty palaces, so he could rest comfortably while journeying from one city to the other. When the southern capital was built, Yang Ti traveled there to inspect it at the head of a fleet of "dragonboats" that stretched nearly a hundred miles along the Yangtze River.

He spared no luxury. When the leaves dropped in the imperial park at autumn, Yang Ti had them replaced with artificial ones of silk. Silken lotus flowers drifted in the imperial lake. Thousands of birds were slain to provide down for his cushions and feathers to decorate the gowns of his wives. So many birds were killed, it was said, that for generations some provinces had none.

Yang Ti did not build simply for himself, though;

he built for his nation. China needed an inland waterway that would bring food from the fertile rice fields of the south to the big cities of the north. A small canal already existed, linking the Yangtze and Huai Rivers. Yang Ti had it enlarged to a width of forty paces. Roads were constructed along both banks and planted with elms and willows. In 606, Yang Ti added a canal from the Yellow River to the Huai, and three years later another one from the Yellow River to the region around present-day Peking.

All of China groaned under the whips of Yang Ti's overseers. But by 610, the first Grand Canal of China was complete. It connected the two capitals of the north with the one in the south and with the rich rice fields. The armies defending the northern border along the Great Wall now would have a steady food supply.

A book written in Yang Ti's time called *Record of the Opening of the Canal* tells us what this project meant in terms of manpower. Some 5,500,000 workers were drafted to work on the Grand Canal. In some places, every able-bodied man between fifteen and fifty was taken. There were 50,000 overseers to supervise their labor. Those who resisted the draft were "punished by flogging and neck weights." Over two million men were said to have been "lost," a total that probably includes those who ran away from the labor gangs as well as those who died on the job.

A man like Yang Ti certainly would want to enlarge the Great Wall, too. If it had not already existed, Yang Ti probably would have invented it. Since the Wall was already there, he had to be content with rebuilding it. In 607 and 608 he added a new section of the Wall east of the upper loop of the Yellow River and finished the extension that his father had begun on the west side of the river. A record of the times says that a million men

92

worked on the Wall in the summer of 607, and half of them died—though here again the runaways may have been counted with the casualties.

Yang Ti, the second Sui emperor, was building for the centuries ahead. He gave China a badly needed canal system, strengthened the Great Wall for hundreds of miles, and defeated the barbarians. These were great deeds. But such projects put a heavy strain on the common people who labored to carry them out. They hated Yang Ti bitterly.

There were threats of revolution, but Yang Ti ignored them. In 614, he led an army of conquest into Korea. This military adventure was a disaster. The Chinese were thrown back with staggering losses. Almost at the same time, the Turks gathered their strength and attacked. Yang Ti, with an army weakened by the Korean defeat, was trapped in a border town when he went to fight the Turks.

With the Emperor penned up against the Great Wall, unable to govern the country, revolution broke out in many places. Seven rival emperors proclaimed themselves. The Sui Dynasty was in deadly peril.

A story has it that Yang Ti was saved by a cunning trick. A Chinese princess who had married the leader of the Turks spread a rumor that the Uighurs, wild barbarians of the north, were attacking Turkish lands. The T'u-chueh prepared to withdraw. At the same time, a small Chinese army led by a sixteen-year-old officer named Li Shih-min was coming to Yang Ti's rescue. Li Shih-min had his men beat drums loudly and wave banners in the air. It looked like a much bigger army than it really was, and the Turks hurried home to defend their own territory.

Yang Ti was free. But the country was in disorder. Instead of doing battle with the seven rebel "emperors," he returned to his southern capital and shut himself up in his palace. He seemed tired and without strength.

One of the self-proclaimed new emperors was Li Yuan, the father of Li Shih-min. His forces invaded one of Yang Ti's northern capitals in 617. The following spring, Yang Ti was assassinated in his own palace. Soon a new dynasty ruled China. Li Yuan became emperor in the summer of 618. But the real power in the land was his son, Li Shih-min, the youthful soldier who had helped rescue Yang Ti two years before.

The new dynasty was called the T'ang. At last, after almost four hundred years, China had a family of native-born rulers who would lead the country for many generations. A time of rebirth was at hand for China under the T'ang Dynasty. New glory, new splendor, were about to unfold.

Ten

The
Rebirth
of China

The first emperor of the new T'ang Dynasty, Li Yuan, ruled only a short while. In his eight years on the throne, he restored order after the civil wars that had followed the downfall of Yang Ti. Then Li Yuan stepped aside in favor of his son, Li Shih-min.

Li Shih-min, who is known in Chinese history by his royal title of T'ai Tsung, may well have been the best emperor China ever had. His reign of twenty-three years was brilliant and glorious. Internal rebellions were put down and enemies beyond the Great Wall were crushed. The harsh laws of Yang Ti gave way to gentler ones. The people supported the government.

T'ai Tsung did not have much faith in the Great Wall. Walls, he said, gave a false sense of security. The proper strategy was to carry the war to the enemy. When a general named Li Chi led a successful campaign against the Turks, T'ai Tsung told him, "You are a more efficient Great Wall than that built by Yang Ti."

T'ai Tsung drove the Turks back and defeated them many times. They submitted to the Chinese Emperor and for many years caused no trouble. A new enemy emerged in the mountainous western land of Tibet, where nomadic tribesmen were united into an ambitious, aggressive new nation. The Tibetans demanded a Chinese princess as a bride for their king. When T'ai Tsung refused, the Tibetans invaded China. The Emperor defeated them in 641. Then he sent the requested princess after all, to ensure peace.

The great Emperor died in 649. During his son's reign, which lasted until 683, the Turks and Tibetans became troublesome again, and the Great Wall had to be repaired and patrolled. Then there were problems within China. Empress Wu, a ferocious old woman, seized power. When her husband, the Emperor, died, she took the throne herself—the only time in Chinese history that a woman has been supreme ruler. She was half insane and put many people to death. Finally, when she was eighty years old, she was forced from control. That was in 705. Within a few years, a strong new emperor, Ming Huang, was in command.

He ruled for forty-five years. It was the high point of the T'ang era. Ch'ang-an, the capital, became one of the key cities of the world, drawing travelers from many lands. In that magnificent city, which occupied thirty square miles and had a population of more than a million, there could be found Arabs, Persians, and Syrians, Koreans and Japanese, men of Tibet and men of Khotan, even some envoys from glittering, far-off Byzantium, and ambassadors from India. This multitude of foreigners brought new ideas into China. After long centuries of isolation, the Chinese were exposed to everything the Western world had to offer.

It was a golden age of art and poetry. The works

of such T'ang poets as Li Po and Po Chu-i are still read and loved today. Porcelain, first developed under the Han, came into perfection. T'ang craftsmen modeled the fierce, snorting porcelain horses for which they are famed and produced the sumptuous and shining vases in glowing greens and oranges that made T'ang ware desired from India to Cairo. Painters, too, achieved wonders. Many of the strange, violently colored T'ang paintings have survived to this day, to our delight.

The T'ang period gave birth to the art of printing, hundreds of years before it was invented in Europe. The Chinese at that time could not use movable type, with a written language containing thousands of characters. Instead, they carved each page on a separate wooden block. The oldest surviving printed Chinese book dates from A.D. 868. The archaeologist Aurel Stein found it in a cave at Tun-huang.

Another invention of the T'ang time was shorthand. An Arab book of the tenth century tells of a Chinese scholar who came to Baghdad to study science. He asked his Arab hosts to dictate the medical books of the great Roman doctor, Galen. "Dictate to me as rapidly as possible," he said. "You will see that I shall write faster than you can dictate." The Arabs read Galen to him "as fast as we could, but he wrote still faster." The Chinese scholar explained to his astounded friends that he was using a system of shorthand, but he said that the system was so difficult it would take an intelligent man twenty years to master it.

Arab accounts also inform us that the Chinese of the T'ang era made use of fingerprinting. "When any contract is entered into," we read, it was usual "for the outline of the fingers of the parties to be traced upon the document. For experience shows that no two individuals have fingers precisely alike." This is not quite how modern fingerprinting works, of course, but the basic idea is close to it.

About 750, the T'ang era was at its most splendid. Then came the collapse, terrifyingly swift. While Emperor Ming Huang surrounded himself with a brilliant court of poets, musicians, and scholars, enemies were gathering beyond the Chinese borders.

The Uighurs, fiercest of the Turkish tribes, conquered Mongolia in 745 and presented a hostile front along the weakest section of the Great Wall, the Ordos loop. To the east, in what is now called Manchuria, a nomad tribe known as the Khitan was moving southward. And in the far west, Arabs were invading the Chinese-dominated city-states of Ferghana, Tashkent, Bokhara, Samarkand.

A terrible battle in 751 saw 50,000 Chinese soldiers slain by the Arabs. The whole western region came under their control. Then Korea and Thailand, which China had ruled for many years, revolted also. While all these uprisings were going on along China's borders, there was a revolution within the country. A general named An Lu-shan, a man of partly Turkish ancestry, rose against the old Emperor and led an army of 200,000 toward the capital. Ming Huang fled and gave up the throne to his son. The new Emperor, Su Tsung, crossed the Great Wall into Turkish-held territory and managed to get the aid of Uighurs and Arabs to put down An Lu-shan's rebellion. In 757, An Lu-shan was killed and Su Tsung returned to his capital.

But T'ang power was broken. Su Tsung had let foreigners pour through the Great Wall. The Uighur armies that had helped the Emperor now began to raid and maraud. Su Tsung had to bribe them to go away, giving them 10,000 rolls of silk and the promise of an annual tribute. The Uighurs halted their attacks on Chinese cities, but they did not go away. They remained as overlords of

China. The T'ang emperors did as their Turkish bosses commanded.

One weak emperor followed another. Two of them met their deaths by drinking poisonous concoctions that they hoped would be elixirs of immortality. When tribal quarrels broke up the Uighurs, another Turkish tribe, the Sha-t'o, replaced them as China's real masters.

By the end of the ninth century the glamor and glitter of the great T'ang days were all but forgotten. Once more the barbarians were taking over. The Great Wall stood useless and crumbling, no longer a barrier against invaders from the north.

The T'ang Dynasty officially ended in 906, when a Chinese rebel forced the twentieth T'ang emperor to give up his throne. Now began the Five Dynasties period, when the imperial title changed hands every few years. A Chinese historian who lived in the eleventh century begins his account of the Five Dynasties period with the word, "Alas!," and that sums it up.

Some of the dynasties were Turkish, others were Chinese. None of them ruled over all of China. The south broke away again, and had ten dynasties of its own within less than sixty years. China was helpless. In Manchuria, the tribe known as the Khitan was getting stronger as China weakened. In 935, the Khitan invaded northern China and overthrew the current dynasty. They put a puppet Turkish dynasty into power but kept most of northeastern China for themselves. The Khitan took control of the best preserved section of the Great Wall, which had long since lacked all purpose of defense anyway.

In the far west, though, the Chinese were still maintaining some sort of order along the Wall. We know this because an Arab traveler, Ibn Muhalhil, made a journey to China about 940 and wrote an account of his trip.

He said that he traveled eastward along the old caravan route until he came to the "Halting-place of the Gate," his phrase for the Great Wall. This was "in a sandy region," probably around Tun-huang. Here, he said, Chinese officers were stationed, and "anyone desiring to enter China from the Turkish countries or elsewhere must ask leave here." After being entertained for three days by the Chinese, Ibn Muhalhil and his party continued toward the east.

In time they came to the "Valley of the Halting-place," where once again they had to ask leave to enter. The valley, described as "one of the pleasantest and fairest regions of God's earth," must have been at Kiayukuan. Ibn Muhalhil entered Kiayukuan, and the rest of his journey was carried out on the Chinese side of the Great Wall.

The Khitan of Manchuria were increasing their power over northern China. In 947, the Khitan ruler proclaimed himself Emperor of China. He called his dynasty the Liao, naming it for a river in Manchuria.

Thirteen years later, a Chinese general named Chao K'uang-yin founded a new dynasty in southern China, called the Sung. The Sung Dynasty was one of the most famous in China's history. But in its 319 years it never had possession of the Great Wall. China was divided, and the barbarian Khitan of the Liao Dynasty ruled the north.

The Khitan were probably descended from the Hsien-pi and T'o-pa nomads of six hundred years earlier. They were herdsmen who measured their wealth in terms of sheep and horses, though they tried to do a little farming where their land was fertile enough.

They were marvelous warriors. A Khitan chief named A-pao-chi had organized them about 907, training a fierce, well-organized cavalry of mounted archers. As they moved south out of Manchuria toward China, no one was able to resist them. They struck in swift raids and followed their attacks with sieges. When they first reached as far south as the Great Wall, in 908, the Chinese defenders were helpless before them.

They captured Shanhaikuan, the easternmost city of the Great Wall. Then they did something really unusual: they built a Great Wall of their own, running from Shanhaikuan northeast into Manchuria. It was an upside-down thing to do—a horde of barbarians extending the Great Wall to protect themselves against the *Chinese* to the south!

But the Khitan did not really need protection. Their advance rolled mercilessly on. After they had conquered most of northern China, the Great Wall cut their territory in two. They kept a capital on each side of the Long Rampart. Peking became their southern capital. It was the first time that that city, which is China's capital today, was important. North of the Great Wall the Khitan had a capital known as Shanking.

They had two systems of government, too. In their original territory the Khitan kept to their old tribal ways. In the conquered part of China they used native Chinese officials, who served to keep the government running in the customary fashion. The Khitan, when they came to rule China as the Liao Dynasty, left the Chinese farmers alone. But they did not understand what was needed to keep Chinese agriculture going. The peasants of China had always had two main enemies, drought and flood. Ever since Shang Dynasty times, the government's task had been to build canals and dams to store water in dry times and keep back floods in wet times. The Liao Dynasty, failing to realize this, did not build any new canals or new dams during the two hundred years it ruled the north of China. Nor did the new masters repair the existing water-control systems. This in time would cause great difficulties for them.

The Khitan had no written language of their own, so they borrowed Chinese writing. But in other ways they tried to keep from being swallowed up by Chinese culture, as had happened to so many other nomad conquerors. They did not succeed. Once they moved south of the Great Wall, the Liao officials and nobles began to wear Chinese clothes, to marry Chinese women, and to adopt many Chinese customs.

In the south, the Sung Dynasty ruled after 960. The Sung emperors dreamed of driving the Khitan back through the Great Wall and reuniting China. But that was a dream that could never come true; the Khitan horsemen were too strong. When the Sung armies went north to attack, they were badly beaten. By 1004, the Khitan became tired of these battles and headed south to invade the Sung domain.

Quickly the Sung emperor bought the Khitan off by paying a heavy tribute. At first it was 100,000 ounces of silver a year, and 200,000 pieces of silk. Then, in 1041, a Tibetan nomad tribe, the Tangut, invaded the western lands of the Sung. The Khitan drove the Tangut out, at the request of the Sung emperor, but charged a high price for their services. The yearly tribute was raised to 200,000 ounces of silver and 300,000 pieces of silk. Soon the Tangut, too, were collecting tribute from the powerless Sung Dynasty.

Though they were hemmed in on all sides by haughty barbarians, the Sung Chinese still felt that they were living in good times. What remained of China was prosperous and happy. By 1100, there were at least five Sung cities with populations of more than a million. Canals and flood-control dikes were built. Merchants from many lands swarmed in the rich port cities. Painting and porcelain making reached their highest peaks of greatness during the Sung period.

It was bitter, though, to know that half of China was ruled by barbarians. The Great Wall itself, the symbol of Chinese power for more than a thousand years, ran entirely in barbarian territory. The rulers of the Sung Dynasty felt compelled to try to defeat the much stronger Khitan.

In 1074, Sung Emperor Shen Tsung began to assemble an army along his northern frontier. He built a Sung "Great Wall" there—not of brick and stone, but of elm and willow trees, which he hoped would slow down the charging Khitan cavalry. Three million trees were planted. A network of canals, ditches, and artificial lakes provided a second line of defense.

The Khitan ordered the Sung to remove these fortifications. The Sung refused, and the barbarians attacked. They were not slowed at all by the trees and the lakes. Only a desperate battle by the Sung defenders stopped the Khitan onslaught.

But the Khitan turned back without going very deep into Sung territory. They were not good fighters, any more. They had lived a settled life too long. Like cautious old men, the Khitan huddled inside their own land and ceased to attack their neighbors. In 1077, they built a new wall along their southern frontier and another one in the north, well beyond the old Great Wall line. They fortified their boundary in the west, where the Tangut of Tibet were causing trouble.

Long ago, the Khitan had pounced like a tiger on China. But now the tiger was old and toothless. New barbarians were coming. They would slay the toothless tiger and take a deep bite out of China themselves.

They were the Jurchen, a Manchurian tribe who

came down out of the forests of the far north. As the Khitan grew weaker, the Jurchen grew stronger. By 1112, a Jurchen leader named A-ku-ta openly defied the Liao Dynasty emperor of the Khitan.

It happened at a feast at a winter camp in Manchuria. The Liao emperor was there, with the nobles of his court. His guests were the tribal chieftains of the Jurchen, including A-ku-ta. The wine bowl passed again and again. The Khitan grew tipsy. The Emperor stood up and ordered everybody to dance. A-ku-ta growled, "I do not know how to dance," and remained seated. The Emperor insisted. A-ku-ta still refused to dance.

A hundred years before, the emperor would have put the stubborn chieftain to death. Now, the Khitan were afraid to start trouble with the Jurchen. Soon, the Jurchen rose in revolt, led by A-ku-ta. They were strong and savage, just as the Khitan themselves had been two hundred years before. In 1115, they captured the northern Khitan capital.

Famine struck the Khitan lands. Their careless policy of allowing dams and irrigation canals to fall into disrepair now hurt them badly. A chronicler of the time wrote in 1118, "the people stripped the bark from elm trees and ate it. Later, men even ate each other." Starving men do not make good soldiers. By 1121, almost half the Khitan empire was in Jurchen hands. The next year, A-ku-ta took the title of Emperor, calling his dynasty the Chin, or "golden." The remaining Khitan fled far to the west. Their days as China's masters were over.

The Sung Dynasty emperor was glad to see the Khitan destroyed. But the new rulers of the north were no friendlier. In 1126 they marched into Sung lands. They captured the Sung capital. The Emperor and all his court, some three thousand people, were carried off as prisoners and taken beyond the Great Wall.

A brother of the captive Emperor escaped and fled

south of the Yangtze River. He kept the dynasty going. But from 1126 on it was known as the Southern Sung Dynasty, because it ruled only over a small part of the former Sung territory. The Jurchen Chin found it difficult to invade the Southern Sung lands. The many rivers and canals of the south interfered with the progress of the nomad cavalry.

In 1141, the Southern Sung emperor signed a peace treaty with the northern conquerors. He agreed to pay a tribute of silver and silk each year and to leave his northern border unfortified. In return, the Chin Dynasty ruler would not attack.

Under the new arrangement, the Southern Sung enjoyed peace and plenty. The rice fields were productive, and no more money and manpower were wasted on foolish military adventures. The new capital city, Hangchow, grew large and grand. Marco Polo, the Venetian traveler who visited it in the thirteenth century, called it "beyond dispute the finest and noblest city in the world," and Marco had seen much of the world.

With the north closed off, China for the first time began to look toward the sea. A Sung navy grew rapidly. The vast Chinese merchant vessels known as junks began to sail to India and Arabia. One Chinese historian wrote in 1178, "The ships which sail the Southern Sea and south of it are like houses. When their sails are spread they are like great clouds in the sky. Their rudders are several tens of feet long. A single ship carries several hundred men. It has stored on board a year's supply of grain."

Wonderful things came from foreign lands: rhinoceros horns from Bengal, ivory from India and Africa, incense, camphor, pearls, crystal, coral, agate, sandalwood, and aloe. The Chinese sent porcelains and silks to other lands in exchange.

Comfortable in their warm cities, the poets of the

Sung time never stopped mourning for the lost lands of the north. Tai Fu-ku, writing at the end of the thirteenth century, spoke for all his people when he lamented:

> How bitterly I wish that mountains blocked my wandering gaze,
> For northwards, far as eye can reach, our conquered land seems endless.

Eleven

The Mongol Hordes

In the middle of the thirteenth century, the English monk Matthew Paris made an entry in his historical chronicle for the year 1240, telling how a tribe of nomads burst out of Asia to invade Europe. They were, he wrote, "like grasshoppers covering the face of the earth, spoiling the eastern confines with fire and sword, ruining cities, cutting up woods, rooting up vineyards, killing the people both of city and country. . . . They are rather monsters than men."

These ferocious attackers were the Mongols. They came out of the region north of the Great Wall of China and speared deep into Europe, reaching Poland and Hungary by 1241 before turning back. But long before the western world had reason to fear the Mongol hordes, these savage horsemen had sharpened their teeth on the flanks of China. Once again, wild men broke through the Great Wall. This time the nomads did something that no earlier attackers had achieved: they made themselves lords of all China, from the Great Wall to the torrid jungles of the south.

As late as the middle of the twelfth century, the Mongols were simple nomads of the far north, drifting from pasture to pasture to graze their herds. Family clans traveled together as units, but there was no real government uniting the entire tribe.

About 1167, a son named Temujin was born to one of the Mongol chieftains. A legend says that when he was only nine, Temujin could ride a speeding horse without touching the reins, showering arrows unerringly in all directions. When he was thirteen, his father died. Temujin had to use strength and cunning to gain his heritage of power. He took command of his clan, then of his tribe, then of all the nomad tribes. The barbarians of Mongolia hailed him as Genghis Khan, "King of Kings."

By the time he was forty years old, Genghis Khan had proved that he was a gifted ruler. He organized the scattered nomad tribes into a solid nation and laid down laws to guide it. His goal was the conquest of all Asia. The richest prize, of course, was China. In 1211, Genghis Khan marched toward the Great Wall.

China was still divided. In the far south was the prosperous, heavily populated Southern Sung realm. From the Yangtze River north to the Great Wall and beyond, the masters were the Jurchen Chin Dynasty. The Jurchen had now ruled for more than ninety years. They were tough, simple-minded warriors who kept aloof from the people they had conquered, using their own language and customs. But lately they, too, had started to show an interest in Chinese ways—always a sign of trouble for nomad overlords.

The Chin emperors grew worried as Mongol strength increased. They protected themselves by strengthening the Great Wall. But that rampart ran through the middle of their domain and could serve only as an inner line of defense. Farther north, the Jurchen rebuilt a wall that the Khitan had originally erected as a defense against *them*. They added a new outer loop, five hundred miles long. In the west, the Jurchen built another wall parallel to and north of the Great Wall, beyond the loop of the Yellow River.

Then they braced themselves for the attack.

Genghis Khan and his Mongols advanced. Though his men were always spoken of as the Mongol "horde," their numbers actually were not great. Terrified victims multiplied the size of the Mongol forces in their imaginations. At the height of his power, Genghis Khan never commanded more than 250,000 men. Only half of these were Mongols; the rest were allies such as Uighur Turks. The whole Mongol population was probably no greater than one or two million. The Chinese at that time already numbered more than a hundred million.

Mongol strength depended on speed and valor, not on numbers. The leather-clad horsemen could ride for days at a time, changing horses without halting. During the invasion of Hungary a Mongol army covered 270 miles in three days, a fantastic feat for cavalry. In battle, they sped forward in flying columns, encircling their foes and ringing them into a panicky herd. The Mongol bows could kill at a distance of two hundred yards. Another Mongol weapon was psychological: cruelty. They would massacre whole cities, not because they enjoyed slaughtering innocent people but because it terrified other cities not yet conquered. The Mongol reputation for murderousness left the enemies half beaten before the first blow was struck. But once they had triumphed, the Mongols were tolerant and justice-loving rulers.

When Genghis Khan began to invade China in 1211, he crossed the 450 miles from his headquarters to the

Jurchen frontier without losing a man. His goal was the Chin Dynasty capital, Yenching, the modern Peking. The Great Wall was at its strongest here in the mountainous country of eastern China. Two walls, from thirty to sixty miles apart, guarded the approach to Yenching. The city itself had huge walls that made the Great Wall look flimsy by comparison. They were forty feet high, topped with hundreds of watchtowers. A triple line of moats gave the city extra protection. Finally, the capital was flanked by four gigantic walled forts, each a mile square, each with its own array of towers, moats, grain-storage towers, and arsenals.

The Mongols broke easily through the outer loops of the Great Wall. But the inner defenses were more stubborn. Again and again the Mongols hurled themselves at the gate of the Wall at Chuyungkuan, north of the capital. They were thrown back every time. The fortress held.

Genghis Khan had split his army, though. A second force of Mongols attacked the Great Wall 120 miles to the west. There, the Wall was guarded by an army of hired tribesmen, the Ongut. When the Mongols arrived, the Ongut saw that it was wiser to join them than to fight. They surrendered without a battle and opened the Great Wall. The invaders burst into China.

The Jurchen troops, who had been guarding the passes north of the capital, hastily turned westward to halt the Mongols. Genghis trapped them and cut them down by thousands in a rain of arrows.

Genghis now circled back, still hoping to break through the Great Wall north of the capital. In September, 1213, his armies pounded against the gate at Chuyungkuan a second time. The gate held. The Wall had been newly fortified with outer trenches. The gate itself, one story said, had been sealed with iron, so that it could not be opened even from within.

The siege dragged on for a month. Then Genghis sent a smaller force, commanded by one of his sons, to challenge the Great Wall pass at Tzuchingkuan, southwest of the capital. The surprise attack worked. The Mongol horsemen roared through the Wall and stormed the fortress at Chuyungkuan from the southern side. They opened the gate to the main army waiting outside.

The way to the capital was clear. But when the Mongols pulled up before the walls of Yenching in 1214, they were shocked at the scope of the task that still awaited them. Who could climb such walls? Who could cross such moats? From the four corners of the city, defenders showered down arrows and crude explosive bombs. For the first time, Genghis began to understand how big China was, how difficult to conquer. He had sent one army through the Wall in the west, and it now held the province of Shansi. After almost three years of siege, he now had managed to enter this eastern providence, Hopei. But there were a dozen such provinces, each with its walled cities. How could those cities be taken? Could China ever be conquered? And, if it could, how could his little band of Mongols ever govern such a vast and populous land?

Genghis hesitated. Two attempts to break into the city were turned back. Then Genghis learned that an uprising was being planned within the city. The Chinese and Khitan subjects were going to revolt against the Jurchen overlords.

Why fight, then? Genghis decided to let the city fall of its own accord. He accepted a Jurchen offer of tribute and collected horses, gold, silver, and silk, along with Chinese princesses, as the price of retreating beyond the Great Wall.

The following May—1215—the uprising came. Traitors handed the mighty city over to the Mongols. Yenching was looted and burned, and its people were slain by the thousands, as a warning to China's other walled cities. The Jurchen Chin Dynasty emperor fled to the south.

Even deeper in the south, the Southern Sung emperor rejoiced at the downfall of the Jurchen. He hailed the Mongols as liberators. He did not think that they would invade his own territory. Barbarians had never invaded the south before, so why should they do it now? They had no use for such hot, swampy country.

Genghis Khan, at the smouldering ruins of Yenching, planned his next step. How could he bring conquered northern China under his control? What was he to do with its millions of peasants and its rich wheat fields?

One of his advisers had a simple suggestion: "Although you have now conquered the men of Han, they are no use to us. It would be better to kill them all and turn their lands back to pasture, so that we can feed our beasts on it."

Another adviser disagreed. He was Yeh-lu Ch'u-ts'ai, a descendant of the old Khitan royal house of Liao. He had been an adviser to the Jurchen emperor. The Mongols had captured him when the Jurchen capital fell, and Genghis Khan had been pleased by his honesty and wisdom. Now this man spoke up: "You have conquered everywhere under Heaven. You can have everything you want, but you have not organized it. You should set up taxation on land and merchants and should make profits on wine, salt, iron, and the produce of the mountains and marshes. In this way China will make you rich. How can you say that the Chinese people are no use to you?"

Genghis saw that it was better to profit from China than to destroy it. He gave orders that the government of China be organized as it always had been and that nothing be done to interfere with the ways of the people. Then he left one of his lieutenants in charge of occupied China and in 1219 went off on another expedition of conquest far in the west. He reached Persia and the borders of India. There, a story has it, a strange one-horned beast came toward him, knelt, and declared, "Prince! Return whence you came!"

The faithful Yeh-lu Ch'u-ts'ai told Genghis not to disregard the warning of the unicorn. "It is a gentle animal, with a horror of slaughter," he said. "Your Majesty has been at war in these kingdoms for four years, now. Perhaps Heaven has seen enough of bloodshed and has sent this creature to warn us to retire." Genghis listened, and in 1224 he halted his westward march.

Three years later he died, at the age of sixty. One of his sons, Ogodai, succeeded him. Ogodai returned to China in 1230 and within four years finished off what was left of the Jurchen realm. China now was divided between the Mongols and the Southern Sung. Ogodai considered invading the south, but it did not seem worth the risk.

The Mongols were spreading out over Asia. Each of the sons of Genghis led an army. Ogodai ruled in China. Chagadai was ravaging Persia and the Near East. Another army was attacking Korea. Batu, the grandson of Genghis Khan, led his men into Europe in 1236. These were the hordes that so terrified the western world. Batu's armies burned Moscow and flooded Poland and Hungary by 1241.

Then Ogodai, the head of the family, died. All Mongol conquests came to a halt. The far-flung princes had to return to their homeland to elect a new Great Khan. That astonished the people of Europe, who had expected the Mongols to conquer every country. Ogodai's son Kuyuk was elected Great Khan, and the Mongols began attacking other lands again. When Kuyuk died, his cousin Mangu replaced him, and by 1259, when Mangu died, the Mongols owned the grandest empire the world had ever seen. It stretched from the Yellow Sea to the banks of the Danube and from Siberia to the Persian Gulf.

They had not tried to conquer the Southern Sung domain. But that rich, strong land had foolish rulers, who rashly attacked the Mongols. That angered the men of the north and led to the overthrow of the Sung Dynasty at last.

When Mangu Khan died in 1259, his younger brother Kublai became head of the Mongol world. Kublai Khan had spent most of his life in China and understood Chinese ways. Now he carried out the conquest of the Southern Sung. The Mongols moved steadily southward.

Kublai was the first Mongol to call himself Emperor of China. He took the title in 1271 and named his dynasty the Yuan, meaning "The First Beginning." For his capital. he built a new city just to the north of the ruins of the Jurchen city of Yenching. The Chinese called this new city Tai-tu, but the Mongols spoke of it as Khan-baliq, "City of the Khan." When Europeans such as Marco Polo began to come to China, they referred to it as *Cambaluc*. Marco described Cambaluc in these glowing terms:

"The streets are so wide and straight that you can see right along them from one gate to another. And up and down the city there are beautiful palaces and many great and fine houses in great number. All the plots of ground on which the houses are built are four-square, and laid out in straight lines. . . .Each square plot is encompassed by handsome streets for traffic; and thus the whole city is arranged in squares, just like a chessboard, and disposed in a manner so perfect and masterly that it is impossible to give a description that would do it justice."

Kublai Khan swiftly finished the mopping-up operation in the south. By 1279 the last Southern Sung emperor was dead. China belonged to the Mongols. For the first time in history, men from beyond the Great Wall were masters of the entire realm.

Kublai Khan reigned in splendor. He had two capitals, one on each side of the Great Wall—Cambaluc, or Peking, and Shang-tu, which westerners knew as Xanadu. He ruled over all of China, Korea, Mongolia, Manchuria, and Tibet. Burma, Java, and Indochina paid tribute. Other members of his family ruled in Persia, Asia Minor, most of the Near East, Russia, Siberia, and Central Asia.

He was a tolerant ruler who drew his staff of advisers from many lands. Christians and Moslems served at his court. When Europeans arrived, they were welcomed warmly. Kublai allowed all religions freedom in his empire. He established public hospitals and orphanages, supported art and science, and collected scholars and engineers about him at Cambaluc. He had the Grand Canal rebuilt and extended northward to his capital city and constructed a highway eleven hundred miles long beside the canal. He did not bother to enlarge or repair the Great Wall, though, since there were no enemies left to guard against.

Though he was kindly and just, Kublai was still a foreigner who ruled China by right of conquest alone. The Chinese people never accepted Mongol rule willingly, any more than they had accepted the Jurchen and the Khitan who had been their masters over the past three hundred years. They dreamed of winning their freedom some day. There was constant talk of an uprising against the Mongols. Kublai had to keep garrisons of Mongol troops near every large city to preserve his power.

For the first time, Europeans began to visit China. A single empire ran the length of Asia, and Mongol discipline made it safe for travelers from the west to enter the oriental lands. Merchants and missionaries set out for the east. The most famous of these were the Polos of Venice.

Venice was the proudest city of thirteenth-century Europe. Venetian merchants went everywhere. Venetian galleys kept the sea free of pirates. The commerce between Europe and Asia made Venice rich.

The brothers Niccolo and Maffeo Polo were dealers in jewels who did business in the Near East. They were on friendly terms with the Mongol rulers, and about 1263 they were invited to visit Kublai Khan. The Great Khan greeted them at his capital and "was greatly pleased at their arrival," according to the account of their kinsman Marco. Kublai questioned the brothers about the customs of Europe and sent them back to their own land, requesting "some hundred wise men learned in the law of Christ" to teach and preach in the Mongol empire. The Polos returned to Venice about 1270.

They were unable to collect the hundred monks Kublai Khan wanted. The Pope provided two friars, though, and rich gifts for the Khan. Niccolo and Maffeo set out for China again. This time they were accompanied also by Niccolo's seventeen-year-old son, Marco.

The two friars became frightened and turned back before traveling very far. The three Polos pressed on through Baghdad and Mosul, through the salt deserts of Persia, and over the "roof of the world" to the oasis cities of Kashgar, Yarkand, and Khotan. Then came the thirty-day journey across the Gobi, that terrifying, haunted desert. They entered China in May, 1275. They had journeyed three and a half years.

The Emperor greeted them in his luxurious summer palace at Shang-tu. Marco was enrolled among the attendants of Kublai and spent long hours telling the Khan tales of the ways of Europe. Kublai appointed the young Venetian as a kind of roving ambassador. Marco went from city to city, collecting information about Chinese customs to feed Kublai's hungry curiosity. Marco covered nearly every province of China: he visited Burma, Tibet, and India; he spent three years as governor of the huge city of Yangchow; he lived for a while at the old Mongol city of Karakorum. Wherever he went, he kept his eyes sharp. Many years later, after he had returned to Europe, Marco wrote it all down in a book that will live forever. He told Europe the story of the land he called Cathay and stirred the wonder of generations of readers.

The name Cathay needs some explanation. It comes from the word *Khitai,* which is what Arab historians called the Liao empire of the Khitan. The Khitan vanished after 1125, but the name somehow lingered on; the Russians to this day call China *Khitai.*

Marco's Cathay was not all of China. The old Sung domain, still being conquered by the Mongols when Marco reached Shang-tu in 1275, is called *Manji* or *Manzi* in his book. The name is taken from an old north Chinese nickname for the southerners: *man-tzu,* "southern ruffians." Marco Polo also occasionally talked of the southern land as Chin or *Sin,* which became China in later European geography books. For a long time no one seemed aware that Cathay and China were two names for the same land. Cathay was a place reached overland out of Central Asia; China was reached by sea. Those who went to one place did not seem to understand the nature of the other. As late as 1661, a sailor named Jon Olafsson, who spent many years in the Pacific, was able to write, "China is a very large and powerful land: to the south of it is India, to the west Tartary, from which it is separated by high mountains and a long wall, said to be 1,000 miles long, which stands between Cathay and China."

Though Marco Polo traveled everywhere in China, he failed to mention the Great Wall at all. That is a major puzzle. Some scholars have said that the Great Wall hardly existed in Marco's time, because it had fallen into such disrepair. But we know that Genghis Khan found the Wall in good shape when he attacked it in 1211. There is no reason to believe that it had crumbled away in less than a century, or that the Mongols had gone to the trouble of tearing it down.

How can we explain Marco's failure to speak of something so conspicuous as the Great Wall of China?

It happens that he neglected to mention a number of important things about China, such as the custom of drinking tea. Perhaps he simply did not have a chance to write everything down. It is said that many of his friends in Venice thought he had exaggerated the wonders of Cathay. When he was on his deathbed, they asked him to correct the book by removing everything that went beyond the facts.

"I have not told *one half* of what I really saw," Marco Polo replied. The Great Wall may have been in that undescribed half.

He did describe a great deal, though. He wrote of Kublai as being "very shapely in all his limbs," having "a becoming amount of flesh," being "neither tall nor short, but of a middle height.' The Emperor's complexion was "white and red, the eyes black and fine, the nose well formed and well set on."

The palace at Cambaluc awed Marco. He tells us, "It is the greatest palace that ever was. The hall of the palace is so large that it could easily dine 6,000 people; and it is quite a marvel to see how many rooms there are besides. The building is altogether so vast, so rich and so beautiful, that no man on earth could design anything superior to it. The outside of the roof also is all colors with vermilion and yellow and green and blue and other hues, which are fixed with a varnish so fine and exquisite that they shine like crystal. . . ."

Marco Polo and the elder Polos had a hard time escaping from Kublai Khan's presence. He found them so useful and interesting that he kept them in Cathay, loading them with wealth and honor but refusing to grant their wish to let them visit their native city once again. Not until 1292, after the Polos had been in China for seventeen years, did Kublai let them go. The homeward journey took them three years. While they were passing through Persia, the sad word reached them that Kublai had died, at the age of eighty. The entire Mongol empire mourned for him and with good reason, for it would never have so wise a leader again.

The Polos reached Venice at the end of 1295. They had been gone so long that no one recognized them at first. They proved who they were but were laughed at when they told tales of China's magnificence. So they invited all their relatives to a banquet. The three Polos were wearing coarse clothes of Mongol make. At a signal they rose and ripped open the seams and linings of their robes, "upon which there poured forth a great quantity of precious stones, rubies, sapphires, carbuncles, diamonds, and emeralds, which had been sewn into each coat with great care, so that nobody could have suspected that anything was there." This dazzling display silenced the doubters.

After three years, Marco went to sea again. Venice was at war with the city of Genoa, and he commanded a Venetian ship. He was captured and flung into prison, which was unfortunate for him but lucky for us. While behind bars he met a writer named Rustichello, who helped him set down the book of his travels. Marco was released after a year and returned to Venice, where he lived in wealth and honor until his death in 1324.

Twelve

The
Ming
Dynasty

Kublai's grandson Timur was now Great Khan of the Mongols and Emperor in Cathay. He was tolerant of Christianity and allowed a priest named John of Montecorvino to establish a Roman Catholic church at the capital. The Pope gave Friar John the handsome title of Archbishop of Cambaluc in 1307. The Archbishop converted Chinese and Mongol children to Christianity, taught them Greek and Latin, and led them in the singing of hymns. Emperor Timur often came to the church to listen to the choir.

But soon Timur was dead, and between 1307 and 1322 six Mongol emperors came and went. The time of Mongol rule was ending. The people were growing restless under the yoke of foreigners.

Travelers still were coming to China, inspired by the tales of such men as Marco Polo. Most of them were merchants. They traveled overland from the territory of one Mongol prince to the next, usually in complete safety.

Abut 1340, a certain Francis Pegolotti of Florence wrote a handbook of travel information and said that the road to Cathay "is perfectly safe, whether by day or night, according to what merchants say who have used it."

Another visitor was Ibn Battuta, a rollicking, globe-trotting Arab from Tangier, who spent twenty-eight years roaming the world, covering 75,000 miles. He got to China in 1347 and reported that it "is the safest as well as the pleasantest of all the regions on the earth for a traveler. You may travel the whole nine months' journey to which the empire extends without the slightest cause for fear, even if you have treasure in your charge." Ibn Battuta entered China from the seaward side, and his travels took him only through the port cities of the south. He knew of the Great Wall, which he called the Wall of Gog and Magog, but he did not visit it and was full of misinformation about conditions in northern China. Ibn Battuta got as far north as Canton and wrote, "Between here and the Rampart, or Great Wall of Gog and Magog, there is a space of sixty days' journey as I was told. This territory is occupied by wandering tribes of heathen, who eat such people as they can catch, and for this reason no one enters their country or attempts to travel there. I saw nobody in this city who had been to the Great Wall, or who knew anybody who had been there."

Ibn Battuta's hazy statement was in error. Northern China was still under Mongol control, and if he had gone north he would have seen not only the Great Wall but the splendid city of Cambaluc, not many miles south of it. Darkness was descending, though. Soon the Chinese would rise to throw off the barbarian yoke. The Mongols would flee; all China would be Chinese again, for the first time since the great days of the T'ang. A silken curtain hard as steel would close the borders. The foreigners would leave, and China would become a land of mystery once more, hidden behind its Great Wall.

The man who overthrew the Mongols was a peasant named Chu Yuan-chang. He was so ugly that his enemies called him the "Pig Emperor." When rebellions against the Mongols began to occur, he joined them, and by 1356 he held the rank of general.

The Mongols retreated toward the Great Wall as the Chinese turned against them. They were heavily out-numbered and no longer had the will to fight back. By 1368 they abandoned Peking. Three years later, the Mongols were chased entirely out of China. The panicky descendants of Genghis Khan fled like sheep before the onrushing Chinese armies.

When Peking fell, Chu Yuan-chang named himself Emperor and called his dynasty the Ming, or "Brilliant" Dynasty. He ruled for thirty-one years. As the first emperor of Chinese blood to hold power over all of China in the past six centuries, he had to reorganize and rebuild the government, rooting out all those who had collaborated with the Mongols. He was a strong ruler, but often a tyrannical one.

After he died, civil war broke out between his grandson and one of his sons, who both claimed the throne. The grandson was the rightful heir, but he disappeared mysteriously. The new emperor was Chu Ti, better known by his reign title of Yung-lo ("Perpetual Happiness"). Yung-lo proved to be a capable and far-seeing ruler, who strengthened the country and kept the Mongols from recapturing it.

One of the achievements of Yung-lo's reign was scholarly: the biggest encyclopedia in history. More than two thousand men worked five years to write it. It contained

11,095 bound volumes, each one half an inch thick, twenty inches high, and twelve inches wide. Piled one atop the other, they would have made a stack over 460 feet high.

There were 917,480 pages, each lettered by hand. The huge book contained all Chinese knowledge from legendary times to A.D. 1400. Only one copy existed at first, but two more were made in 1567. Today only 368 volumes of one set still exist. All the rest were burned during revolutions over the past three hundred years.

Yung-lo began to wage war against the Mongols in 1405. They had been driven beyond the Great Wall, but they were still a threat. A chieftain named A-lu-t'ai was trying to rebuild Mongol power. Yung-lo sent an army to deal with him, but it was defeated.

In 1409, Yung-lo himself led troops through the Great Wall. More than 100,000 soldiers were in his army. A-lu-t'ai's men were surrounded by the Chinese and forced to surrender. But soon there was trouble again. Yung-lo led armies past the Great Wall into Mongolia again in 1410 and 1414. In 1422, Mongol uprisings had to be quelled once more, and this time Yung-lo's army numbered 235,000 men. The peasants of northern China had to contribute 117,000 carts and 340,000 donkeys to carry the army's supplies. Again in 1423 and 1424 Yung-lo pursued A-lu-t'ai, without ever quite catching him. It was on this last campaign that the Emperor suddenly died, after a vigorous and active reign.

One of Yung-lo's acts had been to establish his capital at Peking, the old Mongol capital city. During Sung days, the capital had always been in the south, but Yung-lo moved his court to what was considered a "barbarian" city. The purpose was to be close to the Great Wall, so that he could move swiftly to deal with any Mongol troublemakers.

The Great Wall, which the Mongols had neglected,

had to be reconstructed. Yung-lo built new watchtowers and guardhouses and repaired the Wall itself, from Shan-haikuan in the east to Kiayukuan in the west. The official history of the Ming Dynasty tells us:

"At each transit pass capable of admitting carts and horsemen, guard posts of one hundred men each were established. At the smaller passes for carriers of fuel and herdsmen with their flocks, ten men. The instructions given to the generals ran thus: 'At each signal station let the towers be built higher and stronger; within must be laid up food, fuel, medicine, and weapons for four moons. Beside the tower let a wall be opened, enclosed by a wall as high as the tower itself, presenting the appearance of a double gateway, inner and outer. Be on your guard at all times with anxious care.' Such were the commands of the Emperor."

One travel account of the time tells us something about the state of the western end of the Great Wall in Yung-lo's reign. In 1419, Shah Rukh, the Mongol Khan of Persia, sent ambassadors to China. They took the Old Silk Road eastward, crossing the desert as Marco Polo had done to reach the borders of China.

On August 24, 1420, Chinese officers met them. The next day they were taken to a place where awnings had been erected and an elegant feast spread. A Chinese official counted all the members of the party. (There were 510, including the merchants and servants accompanying the envoys.) On the twenty-sixth, at another desert outpost, the commanding general of a frontier fort was their host at a second feast, placing the envoys at his left. That was the position of honor in China, "because the heart is on the left side." Dishes of meat and poultry, excellent bread, walnuts and pickles, and wine in silver and porcelain gob-lets were put before the Persians. Dancers performed. On the following day, the party continued through the desert and arrived at a strong castle in a valley. This was the gate of the Great Wall at Kiayukuan, the outer limit of Ming Dynasty China.

Here, the entire party was counted again and their names registered, and they journeyed eastward to the walled city of Suchow, within the Great Wall. It took them another four months to reach Emperor Yung-lo at Peking, where they stayed until the following May.

Another traveler, a Turk, gave a similar story of Kiayukuan. He said that the road east into China passed through "an enclosing chain of rugged and steep mountains," and the only way led to a narrow pass guarded by soldiers. There, merchants were asked what they brought, where they came from and how many they numbered. "The answers being given, the Emperor's guards pass it by signal—by smoke if in daylight, by fire if at night—to the next watchtower; they to the next, and so on, till in a few hours the message reaches the Emperor: a thing which by any other means would require many days. The Emperor sends back his orders the same way and just as rapidly, saying whether all shall be admitted, or only a part or all turned away. For the people of Cathay do not approve of the prolonged stay of foreigners among them."

The Mongols also came to the Great Wall peacefully, as tribute-bearers. Every year a delegation of Mongols came to Peking with horses and furs as a sign of submission. Sometimes red tape caused delays at the Great Wall before they were allowed in. When that happened, the Chinese officials had to feed the tribute-bearers at government expense. One Mongol mission, held up at the Great Wall for a month, devoured in that time 3,000 cattle and sheep, 3,000 jars of wine, and 100 large bushels of rice.

After Yung-lo died in 1424 while commanding troops beyond the Great Wall, his body was brought to Peking.

It lay in state for a full year while the court astrologers waited for a proper day for the royal funeral. Then Yung-lo was laid to rest about thirteen miles south of the Great Wall, in a ring of hills that formed a horseshoe around the burial places.

All the later rulers of the Ming Dynasty were also buried there. Their monuments are the famous Ming Tombs. A handsome avenue leads to the tombs. It is lined with giant statues of men and beasts, two by two, in blue limestone: a pair of unicorns, a pair of camels, two lions, and many more. The creatures are awesome and grand. One emperor liked them so much that he thought of collecting them all from the road and arranging them around the place where his own grave was going to be. A court minister, it is said, hurriedly chipped a small piece from each one. That made them unsuitable for tomb decorations, and so they still remain on their majestic highway today. The Great Wall rises in the distance to shield the tombs from evil spirits out of the north.

The emperors that followed Yung-lo were weaker men. A Mongol tribe, the Oirats, gathered strength under a chieftain named Esen. In 1449, Oirat troops broke through the Great Wall at the city of Ta-t'ung. The Emperor, Ying Tsung, was twenty-two years old and a poor leader. He gathered an untrained army of half a million men and hastened to meet the invaders.

At a town on the road between Peking and Kalgan, the armies clashed. The Chinese were routed. The young Emperor was captured by Esen's men. The imperial armies retreated in panic behind the colossal walls of Peking.

Esen was not so foolish as to try to invade mighty Peking. He decided to halt the war and ask for a stiff ransom for the Emperor. To his surprise, the Chinese showed no interest in buying back Ying Tsung. They left him a prisoner, and his brother was put on the throne as Emperor Ching. Esen was welcome to keep Ying

Tsung, it seemed. Puzzled, the Oirat leader went back to Mongolia, taking Ying Tsung with him. After a year he let the useless prisoner go, and Ying Tsung returned in embarrassment to Peking.

Esen's moment of triumph did not last long. By 1455 he was assassinated by some of his own men. The Mongols became divided again and no longer endangered China.

But the Oirat invasion had been a grim reminder of what could happen if the Chinese allowed the Great Wall to weaken. Each Ming emperor in turn put men to work strengthening the Wall. Even so, the Oirats were able to break through it in 1472 and seize the Ordos region as far as the Yellow River. A Chinese army drove them out, and new sections of the Great Wall were added.

The Great Wall was now taking the shape it has to-day. It had become a solid brick rampart topped by elegant battlements and parapets. Along the mountains north of Peking there ran the finest section of all, twenty-five feet thick at the base, fifteen to thirty feet high, fifteen feet across at the top. The Ming emperors spared no effort to keep that part of the Wall in perfect shape. To the west, though, no such wonders were attempted. The Wall there was still a simple rampart of clay and rammed earth, sometimes faced with brick and stone, as it had been in the days of Ch'in Shih Huang Ti.

In 1514, with the tenth Ming emperor on the throne, the "foreign devils" arrived. They were Portuguese adventurers who came by sea. The great age of the European navigators had begun, and for the first time in almost three hundred years there were westerners in China.

The Portuguese did not get a chance to see much of the country. Afraid of strangers and strange ideas, the Chinese refused to allow them ashore. They had to transact their business from their vessels, anchored in the harbor. Even so, the Portuguese found it profitable to trade with the Chinese.

When a new Portuguese expedition set out for the Orient in 1537, it carried a twenty-eight-year-old adventurer who was one of the first Europeans to tell the west about the Great Wall of China. His name was Fernão Mendes Pinto.

Pinto's wanderings took him to Ethiopia, India, Arabia, Malaya, and Indonesia. Sometimes he served as a soldier, sometimes as a doctor, sometimes as a merchant. While on the island of Sumatra he met a man named Antonio de Faria, who had been an honest merchant for a while but now planned to go in for piracy.

Faria and Pinto took their pirate ship through Southeast Asia and up the Chinese coast, looting and plundering as they went. At the port of Ning-po, they heard about an island called Calempluy, where seventeen Chinese emperors were supposed to have been buried amid great wealth. The pirates set off to rob those tombs.

Actually, no such burial island is mentioned anywhere in Chinese records. Pinto and Faria did find an island they said was Calempluy and carried off considerable treasure. But what they robbed seems to have been a Buddhist monastery.

Coming back from this voyage, the Portuguese were shipwrecked and cast up on the Chinese mainland. The survivors set out for Nanking on foot, hoping that there they would find a ship to take them to Thailand. As they marched through the Chinese villages, they identified themselves as Siamese citizens. The hoax worked for nearly two months. They supported themselves by begging food.

When they were still fifty miles from Nanking, they made the mistake of entering the important town of Taiping. An imperial commissioner from Peking happened to be there, and he questioned the "Siamese" suspiciously. They were arrested, flung in jail, and flogged.

For twenty-six days they remained in irons. Then they were taken to Nanking for trial. They were put in jail again, this one a huge place that held four thousand criminals. Finally they came before the judges. One of the pirates explained in bad Chinese that they were neither beggars nor thieves, but honest merchants of Siam who had suffered shipwreck. The judges were not sure what to do and passed them along to a higher court in Peking.

Under guard the Portuguese were sent by boat up the Grand Canal to the capital. They arrived on October 19, 1541. After lengthy legal disputes, the court agreed to release them but ordered them to serve one year at hard labor on the Great Wall before they could leave the country.

Pinto and his companions found themselves being taken to a place he calls Xinanguibaleu—"that is to say," he explains in his book, "the enclosure of the exiles." This was a prison "two leagues square, or little less." A high wall surrounded it, and a broad moat spanned by drawbridges that were pulled up every night. In this place, Pinto informs us, were kept 300,000 men between seventeen and fifty years of age, all condemned to hard labor on the Great Wall.

Pinto says that the Wall had a length of 315 leagues. That is a little more than two thousand miles, which is accurate enough, though he was probably just guessing. "This wall," he writes, "I have seen and measured, being generally six fathoms high, and forty spans thick: and four fathoms runneth a kind of rampart, twice as thick as the wall. . . . This wall or Chanfacau (so they call it, that is, strong resistance) runneth with an equal course till it encounters with hills . . . the wall being only in the spaces twixt hill and hill, the hills themselves making up the rest." (An error, for the Wall travels along the summits of high mountains.)

Pinto reports, incorrectly, that in the entire length of the Wall there are "but five entrances." He apparently had learned of the five most important gates, at Shanhaikuan, Kupeikou, Kalgan, Yenmen and Kiayukuan. But, since he had not traveled the length of the Wall, he did not know that there were many smaller gates.

"At every one of these five entrances," Pinto adds, "the King of China hath one fort and the Tartar [Mongol] another; in every one of the China forts there are seven thousand men, six thousand foot and one thousand horse. . . . In all the space of this wall are three hundred twenty regiments, each of five hundred men (in all 160,000), besides ministers, commanders, and their retinue."

Pinto does not say much about his year of labor on the Wall, and possibly he invented that part of his story. He claims that the Mongols attacked and freed the prisoners working on the Wall, and he describes a visit to the nomad camp. But his tale of life in Mongolia is vague and unreal, as if he made it up out of third-hand reports.

In time, he says, he left the Mongols and marched through western China from north to south. Finally he found his way to Macao, the coastal city near Canton that the Portuguese were using as a trading post. (Portugal still owns it today.) Then, he says, he went to sea again, was shipwrecked, and landed on one of the islands of Japan. If his story is true, he was the first European to reach Japan.

His later adventures were also remarkable. After showing firearms to the Japanese—and wounding a Japanese nobleman in the process—he left and was shipwrecked again, this time in the Ryukyu Islands. Then he was enslaved in Burma, shipwrecked once more off Cambodia, and saw military action in Siam. But by 1558 he was safely home in Portugal. He wrote a huge book of memoirs, telling the story of his travels, but it was still unpublished when he died, at the age of seventy-four, in 1583. Finally it saw print in 1614. It was translated into six languages and published in nineteen editions by 1700. Most of the readers of Pinto's book thought it was a work of fiction, but gradually it appeared that he had been truthful in most details. No doubt he invented a good deal of what he claimed, but it is quite possible that Pinto and his Portuguese companions did indeed toil to strengthen the Great Wall about the year 1540.

Thirteen

Europe Discovers China

The Mongols continued to make trouble. In 1550, nomad warriors broke through the Great Wall near Peking. They spread the kind of terror that China had not known since Esen's raids a hundred years earlier.

The new menace was a chieftain named Altan Khan. The Chinese called him Anda. He put together a federation of nomads about 1530 and within twenty years felt strong enough to attack China. Though the raiders got through the Great Wall without much difficulty, they were unable to do any harm to the walled city of Peking.

Anda's raids went on until the 1570's. Then he tired of the nomad life and built a city outside the Great Wall. The Chinese made peace with him and gave him the title of *Shun-i Wang,* "Obedient and Righteous Prince."

The last Mongol threat to China had ended. The Mongols were starting to become peaceful city dwellers and merchants. They acquired a new religion, Lamaism, and many monasteries opened. Every family sent at least one son to become a lama, or priest, of the new religion. Since the lamas were not allowed to marry, the Mongol population began to drop sharply.

Europeans in ever larger numbers were entering China. The Portuguese had several trading outposts along the coast, and starting in the middle of the sixteenth century Spanish missionaries arrived to convert the Chinese to Christianity. These merchants and priests sent reports of China back to Europe. The western world got its first news of the stupendous Great Wall. This account of Anda's raid on Peking was published in Europe in 1561:

"At the boundary of the kingdom of China, where it borders on the Tartars, there is a wall of wondrous strength, of a month's journey in extent, where the king keeps a great military force in the bulwarks. Where this wall comes upon mountains, they cut them in such a manner that they remain and serve as a wall; for the Tartars are very brave and skillful in war. . . . They broke through a part of the wall and entered into the territory for a month and a half's journey; but as the king prepared great armies of men provided with artful contrivances (in which the Chinese are very crafty) , he kept back the Tartars, who fight on horseback.

"As their horses had become weak and were dying of hunger, one of the Chinese officers commanded a large quantity of peas to be placed in the fields, and thus it was that the hungry horses set themselves to eat against the will of their masters. And in this manner the army of the king of China put them in disorder and turned to drive them out. And now a strict watch is kept on the wall."

The Ming emperor who devoted the most energy to the Great Wall was Wan-li, who came to the throne in 1572. A new barbarian enemy was arising to replace the weakening Mongols. The new threat came from a wild tribe we know as the Manchus. To guard against them,

Wan-li had so much work done on the Great Wall that many Chinese in later centuries thought that he was its original builder. The Chinese name of the Wall, *Wan Li Ch'ang Ch'eng* or "Wall of Ten Thousand Miles," was often taken to mean "Wan-li's Long Wall."

Much of the present Great Wall is Wan-li's work. A new section was built west of the Yellow River, and the eastern part was restored. Inscriptions up and down the length of the Wall describe the building of so many feet of "First Class Wall" here, so many of "Third Class Wall" there. One such tablet records the construction of "two pieces of First Class Wall, each piece 148 tens of feet long plus eight feet, in the Lucky Days of the Winter Season in the Third Year of Wan-li."

Wan-li had good engineers. The well-preserved section of the Wall at the Nankow Pass, the part usually shown in photographs, dates from Wan-li's reign. There, the Wall is built of granite blocks neatly cut to shape. Some of the blocks are fourteen feet long and three or four feet thick. The upper part of the Wall is high-quality brick. Every fifty feet along the fourteen-foot-wide roadway, the Ming builders installed stone drains that carried rain water out of the road and poured it over the Mongol side of the Wall.

When the nomads raided, the Chinese soldiers drove them back, using cannons designed by the Portuguese. These weapons, twenty feet long, were known at first as *Ta Chiang Chun,* "Great Generals," but later they were called *Fo Lang Ch'i,* "Foreign Weapons."

Wan-li was a lazy and superstitious man. Eclipses, comets, sudden floods or droughts all frightened him into thinking that the gods were turning against him. He spent huge sums of money—90,000 ounces of silver for a party to celebrate his marriage, 12,000,000 ounces for the marriages of royal princes, 9,000,000 ounces to build palaces.

Yet there was no money to build dikes and canals. By 1599, the country was almost bankrupt. A few years later, an imperial minister complained, "The treasuries of the provinces are empty. All enterprises are at a standstill. The Emperor himself withdraws from his people. For more than twenty years he has never called a council of his great ministers. The empire is in danger of revolution."

As the Emperor's long reign dragged along, even the Great Wall was ignored and began to fall apart. Many soldiers deserted the garrisons along the Wall, because they were left without pay or supplies. By the time Wan-li died in 1620, after ruling thirty-eight years, the empire was in a state of collapse. Before long, China would once again fall under barbarian rule—this time for nearly three hundred years.

During the closing years of the Ming Dynasty, European merchants and missionaries continued to come to China in steady numbers. The suspicious Chinese would not let them leave the cities of the southern coast, and they got only brief glimpses of the rest of the country. Every scrap of information that these men sent back to Europe was eagerly published and translated into many languages.

The Great Wall fascinated everybody. Each book on China described it. Usually the descriptions were wrong, for few Europeans actually got to see the Wall. They thought it was too big, or that it was too small. Most of them thought that it stopped when it came to lofty mountains, though actually it ran right along the mountaintops. We see this notion in such books as that by the Spanish missionary Juan Gonzalez de Mendoza, who wrote in 1585, "You must understand that four hundred leagues of the said wall is natural of itself, for that they be high and mighty rocks, very close together: but in the other hundred leagues is included the spaces or distances betwixt the rocks . . . made by men's hands of very strong work of stone, seven fathom broad at the foot of it, and seven fathom high."

Mendoza also added this garbled version of the long-ago reign of Ch'in Shih Huang Ti:

"This king, for to finish this wonderful work, did take of every three men one through his kingdom. . . . They almost all did perish that followed that work. The making of this superbious and mighty work was the occasion that his whole kingdom did rise up against the king and did kill him, after that he had reigned forty years."

Friar Mendoza admitted that he had gained his information about the Great Wall at second hand from the Chinese who had seen it. "It is in the farthest parts of all the kingdom, whereas none of us unto this day hath been." But soon the missionaries were providing firsthand details of the Wall, thanks to a remarkable man named Matteo Ricci, the first European in almost three hundred years to take up permanent residence in Peking.

Ricci was a Jesuit priest who came to China in 1582, when he was thirty years old. He had a knack for languages and learned to speak Chinese like a native. This allowed him to win the friendship of many important officials, and he was permitted to enter the northern part of China which had been closed to all Europeans. In 1600, Ricci set out for Peking, where he spent the remaining ten years of his life.

He was a brilliant scholar who had a deep understanding of mathematics, astronomy, geography, and many other sciences. He quickly realized that Cathay and China were not two separate places, as everyone had thought since Marco Polo. Cathay, he saw, was just an old name for China.

The Chinese called Ricci "Li Ma-tou." They asked him to make a map of the world with Chinese captions, because they knew so little about what was beyond their own borders. Their own maps showed nothing but China, with blank space for the outside world.

When Ricci made his map, he carefully put China in the center, so his hosts would not be offended. One of Ricci's Jesuit companions wrote that to the Chinese "the heavens are round but the earth is flat and square, and they firmly believe that their empire is right in the middle of it. They do not like the idea of our geographies pushing their China into one corner of the Orient. They could not comprehend the demonstration proving that the earth is a globe, made up of land and water, and that a globe of its very nature has neither beginning nor end."

Ricci also made astronomical spheres and globes out of copper and iron, illustrating the skies and showing the true shape of the earth. He built a clock that struck the hour on a large bell, which amazed the Chinese. And he translated many books on mathematics and astronomy into Chinese, with the aid of a Chinese convert to Christianity. The Emperor himself, though he did not become a Christian, treated Ricci warmly and gave him many important tasks, such as the job of reorganizing the Chinese calendar.

Ricci probably visited the Great Wall several times, but he did not say much about it in the diary he kept. "To the north," he wrote, "the country is defended against hostile Tartar raids by steep hills, which are joined into an unbroken line of defense with a tremendous wall four hundred and five miles long. To the northwest it is flanked by a great desert of many days' march, which either deters an advancing army from attacking the Chinese border or becomes the burial place of those who attempt the attack."

Though Ricci knew that Cathay and China were the

same place, some doubts still remained. The Jesuit missionaries in India, not knowing of Ricci's ideas, believed that Cathay was a separate country somewhere to the east. They had heard rumors that it was inhabited by Christians descended from the converts made by such priests as Archbishop John of Montecorvino three hundred years earlier.

Actually, the Christianity planted in Cathay around 1300 had long since died out. But the Jesuits of India decided to send an expedition to search for the Christians of Cathay. Its leader was Benedict de Goes, a layman who lived with the Jesuits at the court of the Indian King Akbar.

Goes, born in the Azores about 1561, had gone to India when he was twenty-six. Originally a soldier, he grew deeply religious and joined the Jesuits, though he never became a priest. He was chosen to head the expedition to Cathay because he spoke several Asian languages and had an understanding of the customs of the Mohammedans who occupied most of the land along the route.

The expedition left in January, 1603. Goes raised a beard and disguised himself as an Armenian merchant. He was accompanied by an Armenian servant named Isaac and by two Greeks, a merchant called Demetrius and a priest named Leo Grimanus.

They joined a caravan of five hundred people traveling across the Himalaya Mountains to the city of Kashgar. The trip was slow, for the caravan halted every time word came of bandits ahead. One bandit raid forced Goes and the others to flee into the jungle, but he escaped with his life and belongings. After a journey of twenty days the caravan reached Kabul in Afghanistan. Many of the merchants left the party there. The number of those continuing on to Kashgar was so small that it was unsafe to proceed.

Goes stayed in Kabul for eight months waiting for new travelers to join the caravan. One of those who became part of the group was the sister of the King of Kashgar. She had run short of cash while journeying, and Goes loaned her six hundred pieces of gold to be paid back at Kashgar. When she returned the money, she also presented him with "pieces of that kind of marble which is so highly esteemed among the Chinese." The "marble" was jade, the lustrous green stone that the Chinese love so dearly, which they have always had to import from the west. Goes made good use of his supply of jade later on.

The two Greeks parted from him at Kabul. Accompanied now only by the loyal Isaac, Goes followed Marco Polo's track through the mountains. Bandits and more bandits plagued them. Heavy rains slowed the advance. Many of the travelers froze to death crossing the Pamir Mountains. They were snowed in for six days. But by November, 1603, they reached the city of Yarkand. Goes had to wait here for a full year before the caravan got on the road again. He made good use of his time, acquiring more jade as an investment to take to Cathay.

After many more adventures on the road, Goes halted at another town farther along. The caravan encountered the caravan of the year before, now westbound out of Cathay. The merchants had been to Peking, and they told the delighted Goes about Matteo Ricci and the other Jesuits at the court of Emperor Wan-li. In this way Goes learned that the Cathay he was seeking was the same place as China.

Encouraged, Goes and Isaac separated from the caravan and pushed on together through the oasis towns into the desert that awaited all travelers to Cathay. It was a dangerous trip, for bandits lurked in the region west of the Great Wall, and Goes saw the bodies of murdered wayfarers along the road. But then, after nine days in the desert, Goes' account tells us, they came "to the celebrated northern wall of China, reaching it at the place called Chiaicuon."

This was Kiayukuan, and Goes was perhaps the first Christian to reach it in three centuries. Now that he was at the Great Wall, he had to camp there for twenty-five days while awaiting permission to enter. At last the permission came. Goes could enter China but was not allowed to go to Peking. He would have to stay at the walled city of Suchow, just within the Great Wall.

Benedict de Goes reached Suchow late in 1605, almost three years after he had left India. Both he and Isaac had come through the grueling trip in good health. Goes had prospered, having with him thirteen horses, five servants, two slave boys, and a large quantity of precious jade. At Suchow he met another caravan of Mohammedan merchants returning from Peking. They also told him about the Jesuits there.

Goes wrote a letter to Ricci at Peking, letting him know of his arrival. The letter was given to Chinese messengers. But it was addressed in European writing, which the Chinese did not understand, and it bore Ricci's European name, since Goes did not know what the Chinese called him. So the letter was never delivered.

A year later, Goes wrote again. He was still at Suchow, and now his health was breaking down. He longed to see a fellow Christian again. He asked Ricci to find some way to bring him to Peking.

This letter arrived. Ricci, delighted by the news, chose a Chinese convert, who had taken the Christian name of John Ferdinand, to go to Ricci. The rescuer set out at once on the four-month journey from Peking to Suchow, though northern China was then in the grip of a fierce winter.

Not knowing that help was on the way, Goes was having a miserable time in Suchow. He was a sick man, and he was finding food and medicine expensive. He began to sell off the jade he had brought. Some of his jade was stolen, and he received poor prices for the rest, but he was able to support himself on his profits.

John Ferdinand had left Peking in December. He arrived at Suchow in March, 1607, and found Benedict de Goes on his deathbed. Entering, John Ferdinand greeted Goes in Portuguese. The dying man's eyes filled with tears of joy, and he burst into a hymn. For the next eleven days, John Ferdinand cared for Goes, even cooking some European dishes for him in the hopes of restoring his strength. Nothing could save him. Goes slipped quietly into death.

Though he had not reached Peking, Brother Benedict de Goes had settled the question of Cathay forever. He had passed through the Great Wall—in fact, had died almost in its shadow. And he saw that Cathay was really just the northern and western part of China. One of his Jesuit brethren supplied his epitaph: "Brother Benedict, seeking Cathay, found Heaven."

Not only were men of Spain, Italy, and Portugal entering China at that time, Russians were arriving too. The Russians had been overwhelmed by Mongols in the twelfth and thirteenth centuries and did not gain their independence until the middle of the sixteenth. Now, in search of new markets for trade, they sent men southward into China. The early Russian ideas about China were not very accurate, if we can judge by this startling statement written by a Russian traveler in 1611: "As to China . . . it is completely surrounded by a brick wall, from which it is evident that it is no large place." Soon after, an adventurous voyager named Ivan Petlin set out through Siberia, and he reached the Great Wall in 1620. He observed that the Mongols were allowed to come to the gate with horses to sell to the Chinese but were not permitted to cross into China, except in small numbers.

The Great Wall, Petlin wrote, was "all made of brick of fifteen fathom high [ninety feet!]" And there were "about a hundred towers in sight, on both sides." The towers, he said, stretched as far as the eye could see, and it was four months' journey along the wall to the sea. "In the wall to Cathay are five gates, both low, and straight and narrow. A man cannot ride into them upright on horseback."

Petlin ended his journey at what he called the White City, which was Peking. Wan-li had just died, and his son had begun a reign that would last only two months. Petlin had not brought the proper gifts with him, so he returned home without visiting the new emperor. Soon afterward, the emperor died, and a boy of fifteen took the throne.

Trouble was coming for China. New nomads were on the march.

Fourteen

The Manchu Conquest

This time, the enemy came from Manchuria, the forest-covered northeast. Tribes descended from the Jurchen who had conquered northern China in the twelfth century began to unite. By the middle of the sixteenth century they were clustered just north of China's borders.

The Great Wall, meeting the sea at Shanhaikuan, cut Manchuria off from China. Northeast from Shanhaikuan ran a lesser wall known as the Willow Palisade, built during Ming times to mark the frontier. It was little more than a ditch bordered by willow trees.

On the far side of the Willow Palisade a chieftain named Nurhachi (1559-1626) began to play the role that had been played before him by Mao Tun, Genghis Khan, Esen, Anda, and others: he unified the nomad tribes. In 1584 he had only fifty followers, but six years later he led more than a hundred other chieftains.

His people were not then known as the Manchus. That term was not used until about the time Nurhachi died. It may have come from the name of a Jurchen warrior of early days, Manjusri, whom the Chinese called Li Man-chu. Another suggestion is that *Manchu* is an old word meaning "chief" in the nomads' language.

Nurhachi's people called themselves Aisin Gioro, the Golden Tribe. But soon Nurhachi borrowed the old Jurchen dynastic name of Chin and called his own dynasty the Later Chin. He built up strength carefully, without alarming the Chinese or stirring up his Mongol neighbors to the west. The Chinese still regarded the Mongols as more dangerous enemies than the tribesmen of the northeast. They encouraged Nurhachi, giving him such titles as "Dragon-Tiger General." To them he was a force to keep the Mongols in line, not a threat to China herself. For a long time it had been Chinese policy to keep the barbarians divided by supporting rival chieftains.

Nurhachi was more than just a chieftain, he was an empire builder. He gave up the nomad tent-dwelling life and built a fortified capital just north of the Great Wall. He enrolled many Chinese renegades as advisers and soldiers. By 1616, he gave himself the title of Emperor of the Later Chin Dynasty and claimed the right to occupy the Chinese throne.

Two years later, he invaded the northeastern province of China and conquered it easily. The old Emperor Wan-li was lost in dreams and paid no attention. The weak emperors who succeeded him in 1620 were unable to thrust the invaders back.

When Nurhachi died in 1626, his son Abahai became the Manchu leader. Abahai's army broke through the Great Wall in 1629 and besieged Peking. This threat ended only when the Manchus were in danger of being cut off from their line of retreat. An able general named Wu San-kuei rallied the Chinese troops along the Great Wall. The invaders, afraid of becoming trapped on the

146

Chinese side of the Wall, quickly returned to their home base in the north.

In 1634, Abahai successfully conquered the Mongols with 11,000 men. Now he controlled all the territory north of the Great Wall. The name Manchu came into use in 1635, to refer to all the tribes descended from the old Jurchen. Abahai changed the name of his dynasty from Chin to *Ch'ing*, which meant "Pure."

There were only 300,000 Manchus, but they were extremely powerful. Many Chinese of the border went over to their side, for Nurhachi had set down a policy of welcoming talented men of all nations, giving them high office and rewarding their loyalty generously. In 1633, for example, three Ming generals went over to the Manchus. Later they led armies against their homeland. One of them, Shang K'o-hsi, had twenty-three sons, eleven of whom became Manchu generals.

The Ming Dynasty was tottering. The Emperor had almost no power. The final collapse came in 1644. But when the Ming Dynasty fell, it was not because the Manchus had conquered it. China was undermined from within.

The man who helped shatter the Ming Dynasty and give China to barbarians was an ambitious warlord named Li Tzu-ch'eng. Tall and thin-lipped, with a beak of a nose and a face scarred by smallpox, Li put together a private army of brigands and raided the western provinces of China. He felt that the gods had picked him to found a new dynasty that would rescue the country from the weak, foolish Ming rulers.

Many legends surrounded him. One story says that on a hot summer day he thrust an arrow into the ground and declared, "If I am destined to ascend the Dragon Throne, there will be such a snowstorm tonight that the shaft of this arrow will be covered." Snow fell all night, and by dawn the arrow was hidden in the drifts.

More than 300,000 men were in Li Tzu-ch'eng's army by 1640. He had an almost hypnotic power over his men, and they were fiercely loyal to him. City after city yielded to his powerful forces. Soon he ruled five provinces. At the beginning of 1644, Li named himself as the first emperor of the new Ta Shun Dynasty. In the ancient capital city of Ch'ang-an, he had himself crowned. But there was still a Ming emperor on the throne at Peking.

No invader had ever penetrated Peking's lofty walls. Li Tzu-ch'eng knew, though, that the great capital was full of traitors. Its garrison of 150,000 men was made up mostly of old men and boys. The Emperor was powerless, and the men around him would betray him at the first chance.

Li Tzu-ch'eng's army came down toward Peking from the northwest and attacked the Nankow Pass. Genghis Khan had been unable to defeat the fortress there, but Li Tzu-ch'eng took it without a struggle when the soldiers defending the gate switched sides and surrendered to him.

Moving unhindered to Peking, Li Tzu-ch'eng asked the Emperor to surrender. The Emperor sent to the loyal garrison at Shanhaikuan for reinforcements, but it was clear that they could not arrive in time. On April 8, 1644, the sixteenth and last of the Ming emperors slew his oldest daughter and sent word to his mother and his wife that they should commit suicide. He dressed his three sons in commoner's clothes and ordered them to go into hiding until the dynasty could be restored. Then, toward dawn, he climbed a hill on the palace grounds. "My ministers have deceived me," he declared. "I am ashamed to meet my ancestors." He took off his crown and unbound his long hair. Then he hanged himself from the roof of a nearby pavilion. Never again would a native-born emperor rule China.

In the morning, the gates of Peking were thrown wide, and Li Tzu-ch'eng entered. He gave a solemn funeral to the dead Emperor. Then he rode through the nearly empty streets of the capital in triumph. As he approached the marble bridge that led to the palace, the conqueror halted. He looked up at the five magnificent archways through which only the emperor was allowed to pass. A sign over the gate proclaimed its name: "Gate of Heavenly Peace."

Li Tzu-ch'eng drew his bow and aimed at the word meaning "heavenly" in the inscription. "It is by Heaven's will that I am here," he said. "If I strike the character full center it proves that the empire, All Under Heaven, is truly mine!"

The arrow sped through the chilly air—and missed. Li Tzu-ch'eng hurried into the palace. But he was shaken by the evil omen.

One Ming leader still remained to challenge him. He was the general Wu San-kuei, commander of the garrison at Shanhaikuan. This stocky, hook-nosed man had been born near the Great Wall and had relatives among the Manchus. But, unlike many other military officers of China, he refused to desert to the barbarians.

The story has it that Wu San-kuei was in love with a beautiful singing-girl of Peking, Ch'en Yuen Yuen. When Li Tzu-ch'en captured Peking, this girl fell into his hands, along with Wu San-kuei's aged father.

At once, Li sent word to Wu at Shanhaikuan, telling him of the change of dynasty and asking for his support. He added a gift of silver and enclosed a letter from Wu's father, advising Wu to submit to the new ruler.

Wu San-kuei knew that the Ming cause was hopeless. He agreed to recognize Li Tzu-ch'eng as emperor of the northern and western provinces but wanted to keep control of the east himself. He asked Li to turn over to him the eldest Ming prince, who had been captured by Li. He also asked for Ch'en Yuen Yuen and his father.

Li agreed to most of Wu's proposals. But he left the Ming prince in prison at Peking. And instead of sending Ch'en Yuen Yuen to Wu, Li Tzu-ch'eng kept the lovely singing-girl himself.

Wu was furious. He broke off his understanding with Li and made up his mind to do everything possible to defeat him. That meant making an alliance with the Manchus.

Abahai, the Manchu emperor, had died in 1643. His place had been taken by his younger brother Dorgon, who was acting as regent for Abahai's six-year-old son. Dorgon camped outside Shanhaikuan with a Manchu army, waiting for the right time to invade China. Much to Dorgon's surprise, Wu San-kuei, the commanding general who opposed him, sent him a message of surrender.

Meanwhile Li Tzu-ch'eng was marching toward Shanhaikuan with a large army to bring Wu San-kuei under control. He did not know that Wu was now in league with the Manchus. Li took up a position in a valley south of Shanhaikuan. He planned to lure Wu's men from their fortress, draw back in a pretended retreat, then close in at the sides and shut the trap.

Wu San-kuei led his troops toward the army of the usurper the next morning. Li's men dropped back as planned, then began their encircling movement. Suddenly, to the horror of Li Tzu-ch'eng, a mighty force of Manchu cavalry burst from the hills just inside the Great Wall and roared down to attack!

Li's men panicked and fled as the men of the north once again descended like demons onto Chinese soil. Thousands of lives were lost. Li Tzu-ch'eng barely managed to escape and sped back to Peking. The combined forces of Wu and the Manchus marched now toward the capital.

Seeing that it would be impossible to hold the city against the double army, Li left it early one morning, carrying all the gold and silver Peking contained. Dorgon entered Peking with his Manchu army, while Wu San-kuei set out in pursuit of Li. The gold and silver proved too heavy to carry, and Li dumped the useless treasure into rivers as he retreated. At last only a few dozen followers remained to him. He wandered from town to town, but no one would take him in. When some villagers in the province of Hupei discovered who he was, they killed him.

Wu San-kuei returned to Peking. He hoped to persuade the Manchus to name him as emperor and go home. But the invaders had come to stay. Wu had no choice but to recognize them as the rulers of China.

The young grandson of Nurhachi became the first Manchu emperor of China. Within fifteen years, the last prince of the Ming house was driven from the country, and Manchu control was complete everywhere.

As the man who had helped the Manchus seize the country from Li Tzu-ch'eng, Wu San-kuei was treated kindly by the conquerors. He became enormously wealthy and assembled a private army of his own. Much later, in 1673, ambition got the better of him. He rebelled against the Manchus, hoping to drive them out and take the throne himself. For five years he fought against the conquerors, and after his death in 1678 his son continued the revolt for three more years before being defeated. By 1683, the last rebels were beaten. For the next 150 years, China was at peace.

The Manchus were the last of the long line of China's alien conquerors. They were able to benefit from the mistakes of the Mongols, the Khitan, the T'o-pa, and the many others who had come through the Great Wall. The Manchus did not try to change Chinese life. They used Chinese officials to run the country and kept themselves apart, speaking their own language and never letting themselves become Chinese.

Two long-lived and extremely capable emperors made the Manchu period successful. The first was K'ang-hsi, who came to the throne in 1661, when he was seven. He was the great-grandson of Nurhachi. When he was thirteen he began to rule without the help of regents and proved to be bold in battle and wise in government. He was the emperor who put down the rebellion of Wu San-kuei.

K'ang-hsi saw to it that the Mongols north of the Great Wall would never threaten China's peace. He assigned the tribes to fixed areas, took many Mongols into his own service, and encouraged the former nomads to settle down and grow soft. There were tougher barbarians in the far west, though, the Dzungars, descendants of the old Oirats. When they began to raid Mongolia and the cities along the Old Silk Road, K'ang-hsi personally led an army of 80,000 men to crush them. In a battle in 1696 he ended their threat.

Many Europeans came to K'ang-hsi's court. A number of them were Russians. In 1670, a Russian named Milovanoff crossed Mongolia and entered China at what he called the Stone Wall, which was the Nankow Pass above Peking. He described the Great Wall as being "of gray stone below, but of brick, laid with mortar, above; and in the wall is a gateway-tower with oaken doors sheathed with iron plates. And from that tower, the wall on either side stretches out endlessly; the Manchus said that it goes from sea to sea, and that it takes about a year to ride alongside it."

Five years later, another Russian embassy under Nikolai Gavrilovitch came to China. He wrote, "You can only pass the Wall where gates have been made. Between the high-roads, however, there are other, lesser ones, by which the subject races of China and the frontier Mongols enter the kingdom; for there are many gates in the wall, but it is only over the high-roads that the great caravans can pass."

The Russian traveler Spathary, who saw the Wall near Peking in May, 1676, found it in good condition there, but remarked, "In some places, among the mountains, it has fallen down. The Chinese, speaking of it, boast that when it was built there remained no stone in the mountains, no sand in the desert, in the rivers no water, in the forests no trees."

On his journey Spathary came first to an outer wall, fourteen feet high. A Chinese escort met him there and took him to the gate of the Great Wall. "There, at the first gate, was a great tower, and at the gate stood the governor of the town, counting all who passed, for such is their custom. And not only the people, but the arms they carry; all which is written down, lest any other man or weapon should pass when these return. And this they do not only at these gates, but at all gates in the Great Wall." He passed through the first gate, which was twenty-eight feet wide and defended by a guard. Twenty-eight yards farther on was a second wall with similar gates, and beyond that a third. "And all those gates and towers are very strong," he wrote, "the third (inner) wall thicker than the others, and all three are built across the stony ravine about fifty-six feet wide, with a high and rocky cliff on either side. The doors themselves in the gate towers are sheathed with iron."

The Jesuits, who had come to Peking at the beginning of the seventeenth century, had remained there during the collapse of the Ming Dynasty. K'ang-hsi made use of their scientific skills. They built cannons and forecast eclipses for him, and he sent them on long missions of exploration. Some time before 1694, one Father Alexander toured the Great Wall from west to east at K'ang-hsi's command. He reported that parts of it were so wide that eight horsemen could comfortably ride abreast on it.

In 1708, K'ang-hsi sent several other Jesuits to survey all of China. They followed the outer line of the Great Wall from Shanhaikuan to Suchow, then went south to map some of the inner spurs. The map of the Wall that they produced was fifteen feet long. The Jesuits found the Wall in good repair in the east, but, as one of them wrote, "Along the northern border of Shansi the Wall is made of clay, without battlements, and is only about five feet high. West of Shansi it is a narrow mud rampart, sometimes even only a sand ridge."

When K'ang-hsi died in 1722, after a reign of sixty-one years, he left thirty-five sons. He had named no successor. One of his many sons made himself emperor. For his own safety, he exiled or arrested most of his brothers. Since some of the imperial princes had become Christians, the new emperor turned against that religion. He ordered all the missionaries confined either to Peking or Macao. He did not expel them from China, but he would not allow new priests to enter.

He was followed by a great ruler, Ch'ien-lung, the grandson of K'ang-hsi. Ch'ien-lung began to rule in 1735, when he was twenty-five years old. He was a shrewd, courageous, highly intelligent monarch. On the battlefield he was heroic. When the wild Dzungars of the far west became unruly, Ch'ien-lung attacked them with his army and killed nearly a million of them, smashing their strength forever. He conquered Tibet and other lands bordering China and put together an empire even greater in size than that of T'ang days. A chronicler of Ch'ien-lung's time wrote, "The empire was at peace. On the frontiers no more fires were lit in the watchtowers of the Great Wall announcing alarm."

Ambassadors from many European countries came to China during the eighteenth century. They were eager to do business with the Chinese and wanted the Emperor's permission to engage in international trade.

Most of these embassies accomplished nothing. Ch'ien-lung felt that China had no need to do business with foreigners. Some of the ambassadors offended the Emperor by refusing to bow and kneel before him in the customary fashion. Even when they did humble themselves, it did little good. One Dutch ambassador bowed so hard his wig fell off, and he seemed more like a clown than a diplomat to the suave Ch'ien-lung.

In 1792, the first English embassy to China set out. Its leader was an experienced diplomat, George Macartney. He was instructed to negotiate a treaty of commerce and friendship between England and China and to bring back every kind of information about life in Ch'ien-lung's land.

Macartney took ninety-five persons with him, not only diplomats and interpreters but an artist, a watchmaker, a maker of mathematical instruments, five German musicians, and a botanist. After a long sea journey, they docked at the port of Tientsin in the summer of 1793, and set out for Peking.

Chinese court officials met the visitors. They explained to Macartney the requirement that all who came before the Emperor must perform "the three kneelings and the nine knockings of the head." Macartney told them plainly that he would bend one knee before Ch'ien-lung, as he would before King George III, but would go no farther. The officials were unhappy about this, but it turned out that Ch'ien-lung was not bothered by the omission.

The envoys reached Peking in August, 1793. Ch'ien-lung was at the summer palace north of the Great Wall. Macartney was glad to have a chance to see the famous Wall. On September 5, the travelers arrived at the Great Wall at the Kupeikou Pass. Here, rocky mountains rose steeply from the plain. The road ran through a narrow ravine between the mountains.

They found the Great Wall in need of repair. The gates were open, and some were in ruins. Macartney noted in his journal that the Wall was "built of blueish colored brick, not burnt but dried in the sun, and raised upon a stone foundation." He measured the Wall as twenty-six feet high and calculated the number of bricks it contained.

One of Macartney's men took some samples of the brickwork to find out why it was blue. Later he reported that experiments showed that the color came from iron in the original clay and in the ashes and coal used to bake the bricks. This showed Macartney that he had been wrong to say that the bricks had been dried in the sun, and he admitted they had been baked in a kiln.

Macartney measured the openings along the top of the Wall. He found a series of holes a foot long and ten inches wide. They were too small to aim bows and arrows through, but just right for men armed with rifles. He had heard that the Great Wall had been built about 200 B.C., and that led him to think that the Chinese must have had rifles in Ch'in Shih Huang Ti's time, sixteen centuries before they were first used in Europe. What he did not know was that this particular section of the Wall had been built in Ming times and was less than two hundred years old.

The Great Wall, Macartney thought, "is certainly the most stupendous work of human hands." He praised its builders for their wisdom and foresight in constructing the vast barrier against invaders. But he noted that the

Great Wall was now "falling fast to decay, very little care being taken to preserve it." China no longer had need of it, he said, "for the Emperor now reigning has extended his territory so far beyond it."

On September 14, the English envoys came before Ch'ien-lung. The Emperor was eighty-three years old, but, Macartney wrote, "he is a very fine old gentleman, still healthy and vigorous, not having the appearance of a man of more than sixty." They presented him with telescopes, vases, clocks, and other products of European art and sciences. In turn they received gifts from the Chinese. Macartney was given "a whitish, agate-looking stone about a foot and a half long, curiously carved, and highly prized by the Chinese . . . to me it does not appear in itself to be of any great value."

The mission was a failure. Ch'ien-lung was polite and gracious, but he did not want to do business with England. "Strange and costly objects do not interest us," he declared. "As your ambassador can see for himself, we possess all things. We set no value on objects strange and ingenious and have no use for your country's manufactures." Early in 1794, Macartney and his party set out unhappily for home. Though he had not secured the treaty he wanted, the mission aroused great interest in Europe. Many members of the group published books about China, and suddenly everyone in England was collecting Chinese vases and decorating his home in a Chinese style.

In 1795, Ch'ien-lung stepped down from the throne. He said he had ruled for as many years as the great K'ang-hsi and did not wish to hold the throne longer than his famous grandfather. He died in 1799, nearly ninety years of age.

The Manchu emperors who followed him were weak. Flood and famine struck China. Rebellions were constant. There were no more invasions from beyond the

Great Wall, for all the barbarians by now were part of the empire. But invaders came by sea, Germans and French and English who carved China up as they pleased and ran the country for their own private profit. It was a peaceful invasion, for China was too feeble to keep the merchants out. In 1912 the end came for the Manchus. The Ch'ing Dynasty was swept away to join the Ch'in and the Han and the T'ang and the others in the history books. This time there was no new dynasty to take its place. After twenty-two centuries as an empire, China became a republic. How strange that would have seemed to Ch'in Shih Huang Ti!

Fifteen

The
Nineteenth Century
and After

With China in the hands of European business interests from the middle of the nineteenth century on, tourists from the west arrived in droves. Nearly all of them went to Peking, then saw the Ming Tombs and visited the Great Wall. But only a few, like the bold archaeologist Aurel Stein, ventured into the bandit-infested northwest.

At the end of the century, the tourist traffic was halted by the bloody uprising known as the Boxer Rebellion. Hundreds of Europeans were killed in this angry revolt by China against the "foreign devils."

Oddly, the Great Wall is said to have figured in the outbreak of the Boxer Rebellion. According to a story some writers tell, four bored newspapermen in Denver began it all.

The four had gone to a railroad station to interview some visiting celebrity. The celebrity did not arrive. The reporters needed a story, so they made one up. They cooked up a wild tale, writing that some American engineers had stopped off in Denver on their way to China. The mythical engineers, it seemed, had been hired to tear down the Great Wall of China. Demolishing the Wall would be a sign of Chinese good will, showing that all foreigners were welcome there.

The stories appeared the next day, under headlines like these:

GREAT CHINESE WALL DOOMED!
PEKING SEES WORLD TRADE!

Newspaper readers in Denver knew it was a joke. But the story got to China, and the Chinese took it seriously. They heard it in a twisted form. Chinese papers shrieked the word that Americans were coming to force China to tear down its national monument, the Great Wall! Already simmering with revolt after half a century of European greed, the Chinese rebels could no longer control themselves. Furious fighting broke out. Hundreds of missionaries were butchered all over China, and by June, 1900, the foreign embassies at Peking were under siege.

Two months later, an international army from Germany, Japan, France, Great Britain, Russia, and the United States invaded China and put down the uprising. Much of Peking was burned in the battle, and an untold number of Chinese were slaughtered.

When order was restored, the sightseers and archaeologists returned. By 1923, at least three westerners had completed the tour of the Wall from one end to the other. The first was William Edgar Geil, who made the trip about 1908. During the First World War, a much more careful observer, Frederick G. Clapp, made the journey with several companions and reported on it in 1920 to the American Geographical Society. Soon after, a traveler named Adam Warwick explored the Wall, telling the readers of the *National Geographic Magazine* about it in 1923.

Geil began his tour at Shanhaikuan. He noted that there was talk of building a railroad pass through the Wall at that point but doubted that it would ever be done, calling it "a cruel sacrilege to pierce the Great Wall with an iron track." It was done, though, late in 1909, not at Shanhaikuan but farther west at the Nankow Pass. Tunnels, one of them almost four thousand feet long, passed under the Great Wall. The tracks in one place went through the Wall at the opening made, according to legend, by the weeping Meng Chiang Nu.

The Nankow Pass near Peking was probably the section of the Wall visited most often by western tourists. One of them was Romyn Hitchcock, who in 1891 told the readers of the *Century Illustrated Monthly Magazine* that "formerly the Nankow Pass was the great commercial highway to and from Mongolia. It was then an excellent stone road, laid with great blocks of granite, or cut into the rocky hills, over which carts could travel. It is now a rough and almost dangerous path, where carts do not attempt to pass; the merchandise is still transported on pack animals—ponies, mules, donkeys, and camels—and of these there is an endless succession of caravans from dawn till sunset." Frederick Clapp, thirty years later, described the pass as "wild and gloomy, bounded by towering crags, scarcely leaving room for the stony torrent and the railroad." He remarked that the caravan traffic was no longer to be seen, now that the railroad ran through the Great Wall at Nankow.

Travelers who saw the Wall farther to the west wrote sadly of its decay. Orvar Karlbeck, a Swedish dealer in Chinese art, toured the western Wall in the 1920's and wrote, "instead of withstanding the onslaught of sand-storms it had crumbled to insignificance" because "it had been cast from loess but not faced with brick." He reported that "the watchtowers, however, were so faced and were in quite good repair."

Those who tried to follow the Wall through the Ordos Desert had an unpleasant chore. Two travelers who passed that way in 1912, R. S. Clark and A. de C. Sowerby, hardly make the Ordos sound appealing:

"The country . . . is wild and inexpressibly dreary. Very few trees are to be seen, and the bare brown cliffs and yellow sand are devoid of any vegetation, save an occasional tuft of some sage scrub. In places, especially where, as in the northeast, it rises to any prominence, gloomy chasms, with deadly quicksands lurking in their depths, gape in the sandstone and the half-formed shale. To north and west the prospect is heartbreaking. Sand dunes and sand dunes and again sand dunes shifting with every storm and obliterating every landmark. Only here and there, as tiny islands in a sea of desolation, small clusters of mud huts, where some little oasis marks the site of a spring or well."

Frederick Clapp, who tried to survey the Wall in this region about 1917, ran into a problem. Many emperors since Ch'in Shih Huang Ti had built boundary walls across the Ordos at different points. Which was the real Great Wall? Clapp tells how he came to the ruins of a desert wall which all existing maps recorded as the Great Wall. But the natives said, "This is *not* the Great Wall; this is the First Frontier Wall, built only four hundred years ago; the Great Wall is farther north." Clapp decided that "the ruins of the real Great Wall lie buried in the desert sands somewhere in the Ordos."

Adam Warwick, visiting the same area a few years later, described the Wall as "An earth and gravel mound a few feet high, [its] once historic towers . . . now merely rubbish heaps. . . . There is little if any interest in following this crumbling mound, hastily thrown together, of materials collected on the spot by the builders, who made scarcely any effort to encase it in granite or protect it or embellish it with parapets. The traveler here finds many difficulties without an adequate reward."

William Edgar Geil, following this ruined section of the Wall toward its western end, wrote, "Its course is in a wide and lofty valley, over broken hills and upon mountains." He asked a native why the people did not repair the Great Wall and was told, "We cannot repair our own city, how then the Great Wall?" But farther on, as the Wall neared Kiayukuan, it was in good condition. Geil wrote of Kiayukuan "with its embattled walls and three-storied towers" and said that it "appeared very beautiful to a wearied traveler who for weeks past had wandered over the desert."

The best description of Kiayukuan, perhaps, is that of the archaeologist Aurel Stein. He approached it from the outside after his explorations in the desert west of the city. In July, 1907, after his work at Tun-huang, Stein rode toward Kiayukuan. "Looking down from a height of close on 8,000 feet I could see distinctly the low gravel ridges closing the valley at its eastern end, and above them a faint white line lit up by the setting sun—the long-expected 'Great Wall.' The distance separating me from it was still over twenty miles. Yet I thought that I could make out towers reflecting the slanting rays and beyond them a great expanse of dark ground, the fertile district of Suchow." The next day, after crossing "four miles of stony waste, slightly but steadily rising," Kiayukuan came into sight again. "The many-storied gate tower built in wood first became visible; then, as we got nearer, the clay wall which stretches away on either side of the square fort guarding the great gate." The gates of the Wall opened for him, and the distinguished archaeologist entered Cathay.

Today China has strange new masters. The Communist rulers look to east and west to find their enemies, but they no longer need to fear nomads of the north. Manchuria and Inner Mongolia are now Chinese provinces. Millions of Chinese settlers have changed the nature of those one-time nomad territories. Outer Mongolia, further to the north, still has a large nomad population, but there is no chance of an invasion of China such as happened under Genghis Khan.

The Communist government of China does not invite tourists from non-Communist countries to enter. Americans are completely banned from China, but some visitors from neutral and Communist nations still are allowed in. One section of the Great Wall north of Peking has been rebuilt as a showplace for these visitors.

A western newspaperman saw the restored section of the Great Wall in 1962. New brickwork made the Wall seem as majestic as it must have looked during the days when it was an active line of defense. But a sign decreed sternly, "Foreigners not allowed beyond this point without special permission." The correspondent was able to see that "the ancient stones are crumbling and overgrown as the Wall stretches away." Beer was served and music was played during the visit.

So the Wall seems to have come to the end of its long career. No longer a barrier against grim warriors of the north, it is now a tourist attraction. Thousands of scribbled signatures and slogans have been written on it. Someone has scrawled in western writing on the face of the Great Wall of China the inscription, *"Viva Castro!"*

William Edgar Geil once wrote, "The Wall is not for

modern use. It is an ancient fossil—the largest fossil on the planet." There it stands, crumbling and pathetic, a weathered hulk centuries old. It was designed to turn back invaders. Yet barbarians ruled China for some 850 out of the last 1,500 years. Only in the T'ang and Ming Dynasties was all of China under Chinese control. The rest of the time, invaders were triumphant.

But was the Wall really so futile? Time and again the invaders were swallowed up by the civilization they had conquered. "China is a sea which salts all the streams that flow into it," an old proverb says. We have seen how the T'o-pa, the Khitan, and many of the other conquerors found it impossible to resist the lure of Chinese ways.

Maybe the Great Wall really was, as one writer calls it, "the greatest example of wasted military effort in the history of the world." But the Wall has always been more than just a mighty barrier; it has been the symbol of China. The Great Wall draws a line of stone between China and the outer darkness of the barbarian countries. The story of China is the story of the magnificent Long Rampart that set her apart from the world.

Index

Abahai (Manchu emperor), 146–147, 150

Akbar (Indian king), 139

A-ku-ta (Jurchen chieftain), 104

Altan Khan, *see* Anda

An Lu-shan (T'ang general), 98

Anda (also known as Altan Khan), 133–134, 145

Arabia, 81, 105, 129

Bactria, 66, 69

Batu (Mongol general), 113

Bokhara, 98

Boxer Rebellion, 159–160

Buddhism, 87–88, 129

Burning of the Books, 44–45, 47, 51

Byzantium, 89, 96

Cambaluc (also known as Khanbaliq), 114–115, 118, 122

Canton, 122, 131

Cathay, derivation of name for China, 117

Chagadai (Mongol leader), 113

Chang Ch'ien (Han explorer), 65–67

Chang Tsai, 84

Ch'ang-an, city of, 91, 96, 148

Chao (king of Ch'in), 18, 20, 28

Chao, state of, 15, 17, 20, 26, 28, 47

Chao Chun, 75–76

Chao Kao (Ch'in statesman), 47–50, 53–56

Chao K'uang-yin (Sung emperor), 100

Chao Ti (Han emperor), 64

Ch'en Yuen Yuen, 149–150

Cheng (king of Ch'in), *see* Shih Huang Ti

Ch'i Dynasty, Northern (550–577 A.D.), 88–89

Ch'i, state of, 6, 10–11, 14–17, 20, 28–29

Ch'ien-lung (Ch'ing emperor), 154–157

Chin, state of, 10–11, 14, 20

Chin Dynasty (265–317 A.D.), 83–84

Chin Dynasty (1125–1134 A.D.), 104–105, 108, 110–112, 146

Chin Dynasty, Later, *see* Ch'ing Dynasty

Chin Mi-ti (Hsiung-nu prince), 64, 74

Ch'in, state of, 10–11, 15–20, 26, 28–30

Ch'in Dynasty (221–207 B.C.), 21, 25, 46, 56–58, 158

Ch'in Shih Huang Ti, *see* Shih Huang Ti

Ching Ti (Ming emperor), 127

Ch'ing Dynasty (1644–1912 A.D.), 146–158

Chou, state of, 6, 17

Chou Dynasty (1027–256 B.C.), 6–9, 16–17, 20, 57, 65

Chou Dynasty, Northern (557–589 A.D.), 88–90

Christianity, 115, 121, 134, 138, 141, 154

Chu Ti (Ming emperor), *see* Yung-lo

Chu Yuan-chang (Ming emperor), 123

Ch'u, state of, 15–17, 19–20, 28

Chuan-hu (Hsia emperor), 4

Chu-jung, 4

Chuyungkuan, city of, 110–111

Clapp, Frederick, 160–162

Clark, R. S., 162

Dorgon (Manchu regent), 150–151

Dynasty, definition of, 4

Dzungars (tribe), 152, 154

Egypt, vii–viii, x–xi, 1–2, 81

Erh Shih Huang Ti (Ch'in emperor), 47–48, 53–54, 56

Esen (Oirat chieftain), 127–128, 133, 145

Fa-hsien (Buddhist pilgrim), 87

167

Fan San-lang, 39–40
Faria, Antonio de, 129–130
Feng shui (science of winds and waters), 50
Ferdinand, John, 141–142
Ferghana, 66–69, 98
Five Dynasties period, 99
Five Sovereigns, 4
Fu Hsi, 4
Fu Su (prince of Ch'in), 47–48, 50, 55

Gavrilovitch, Nikolai, 152–153
Geil, William Edgar, 34, 160–161, 163–165
Genghis Khan (Mongol Great Khan, also known as Temujin), 108–113, 118, 123, 145, 148, 164
Gobi Desert, 6, 35, 67, 87, 116
Goes, Benedict de, 139–142
Gog and Magog, 122
Grand Canal, 92, 115, 130
Great Wall of China:
  cause of Boxer Rebellion, 159–160
  constructed by Meng T'ien, 28–33
  described by Macartney, 156–157
  described by Mendoza, 136–137
  described by modern travelers, 160–165
  described by Petlin, 142–143
  described by Pinto, 130–132
  described by Ricci, 138
  described by Spathary, 153
  extended by Han Wu Ti, 68–70
  extended by the Khitan, 101
  extended by Northern Ch'i Dynasty, 88–89
  legends of, 37–42
  penetrated by the Mongols, 109–110
  projected by Shih Hung Ti, 25–28
  rebuilt by Chin Wu Ti, 84
  rebuilt by Sui Dynasty, 90–94
  reconstructed by Ming Dynasty, 124–125, 128
  reconstructed by the T'o-pa, 86

rediscovered by Aurel Stein, 70–72
restored by Wan-li, 134–136
Grimanus, Leo, 139

Han, state of 15, 17, 20, 28
Han Dynasty (202 B.C.–9 A.D.; 25–220 A.D.), 56, 59, 65, 71, 77–79, 81, 158
Hangchow, 105
Hitchcock, Romyn, 161
Hopei, 111
Horses, 67–68
Hou Ching (T'o–pa general), 89
Hsia Dynasty (1994–1523 B.C.), 4–5
Hsien-pi (tribe), 84–85, 88, 100
Hsien-yang, city of, 22, 46, 49, 55
Hsin Dynasty (9 B.C.–23 A.D.), 78
Hsiung-nu (tribe), 27, 57–61, 63–69, 73–79, 83
Hsuan Ti (Northern Chou emperor), 90
Hsuan Wang (Chou king), 7–8
Hu (tribe), *see* Tung-hu
Hu Hai, *see* Erh Shih Huang Ti
Huai River, 92
Huang Ho, *see* Yellow River
Huang Ti (the Yellow Emperor), 4
Huns, 84–86
Hupei, 151

Ibn Battuta (Arab traveler), 122
Ibn Muhalhil (Arab traveler), 99–100
Ili Valley, 66–67
India, 70, 87–88, 96, 105, 113, 116, 129, 139, 141
Indian Ocean, 81
Islam, *see* Moslems

Jesuits, 137–141, 153–154
John of Montecorvino (Archbishop of Cambaluc), 121, 138
Juan-juan (tribe), 86–87, 89
Jung (tribe), 9, 16
Jurchen (tribe), 103–105, 108–113, 115, 145–147

Kalgan, 86, 127, 131

Kan Ying, 80
K'ang-hsi (Ch'ing emperor), 152–154
Kao-Sin (Hsia emperor), 4
Karakorum (Mongol capital), 117
Karlbeck, Orvar, 161–162
Kashgar, 69, 116, 139–140
Khan-baliq, see Cambaluc
Khitan (tribe), 98–104, 109, 111–112, 115, 117, 151 165
Khotan, 87, 96, 116
Kiayukuan, 33–35, 43, 65, 68, 70, 80–81, 100, 125–126, 131, 141, 163
Kublai Khan (Mongol Great Khan and Yuan emperor), 114–116, 118–119, 121
Kupeikou Pass, 131, 156
Kuyuk Khan (Mongol Great Khan), 113–114

Lamaism, 133–134
Li Kuang-li (Han general), 68
Li Ling (Han general), 73–74
Li Po (T'ang poet), 97
Li Shih-min, see T'ai Tsung (T'ang emperor)
Li Ssu (Ch'in adviser), 18–21, 28, 43–45, 47–49, 53
Li Tzu-ch'eng (Ta Shun emperor), 147–151
Li Yuan (T'ang emperor), 94–95
Liangchow, 33
Liao Dynasty (907–1125 A.D.), 100–104, 112, 117
Liu Hsiu (Han emperor), 79
Liu Pang (Han emperor), 55–60, 79
Liu Pei (Han warlord), 82
Loess, composition of, 3
Loyang, city of, 91
Lu (Han empress), 60
Lu, state of, 6, 10, 16
Lu Pu-wei (Ch'in adviser), 18–19

Macoa, city of, 131, 154
Macartney, George, 155–157
Manchu Dynasty (1644–1912 A.D.), see Ch'ing Dynasty
Manchuria, 14–15, 27, 65, 98–101, 103–104, 115, 145, 164

Manchus (tribe), 134, 145–158
Mangu Khan (Mongol Great Khan), 114
Mao Tun (Hsiung-nu chieftain), 58–59, 145
Mendoza, Juan Gonzales de, 136–137
Meng I, 29, 46–47, 49–50
Meng Chiang Nu, 39–41, 161
Meng T'ien (builder of Wall), 28–33, 45, 47–50, 58
Ming Dynasty (1368–1644 A.D.), 123–128, 134–136, 145, 147–149, 151, 153, 156, 165
Ming Huang (T'ang emperor), 96, 98
Ming Ti (Han emperor), 79
Ming Tombs, 127, 159
Mohammedans, see Moslems
Mongolia, 14, 27, 59, 67, 73, 89, 98, 115, 124, 128, 131, 152, 161, 164
Mongols, 107–119, 121–128, 131, 133–135, 142, 146–147, 151–152
Moslems, 115, 139, 141
Mu Wang (Chou king), 65

Naking, 84, 129–130
Nankow Pass, 135, 148, 152, 161
Ning-po, city of, 129
Nurhachi (Manchu emperor), 145–147, 151–152

Ogodai Khan (Mongol Great Khan), 113
Oirats (tribe), 127–128, 152
Olafsson, Jon, 117
Ongut (tribe), 110
Ordos Desert, 27, 64–65, 98, 128, 162

Pamir Mountains, 140
Pan Ch'ao (Han general), 80–81
Pao Ssu, 8–9
Paris, Matthew (English monk), 107
Parthia, 69, 80
Pegolotti, Francis, 122
Peking, 31, 86, 101, 110–112, 114–115, 123–124, 126–129, 133–134, 137, 140–143, 146, 148–155, 159–161, 164

Persia, viii, 89, 113, 115–116, 119, 125
Petlin, Ivan, 142–143
Pinto, Ferñao Mendes, 129–132
Po Chu-i (T'ang poet), 76, 97
Polo, Maffeo, 116, 119
Polo, Marco, 70, 105, 116–121, 125, 137, 140
Polo, Niccolo, 116, 119
Portuguese, 128–132, 134–135, 142

Record of the Opening of the Canal (K'ai Ho Chi), 92
Ricci, Matteo, 137–138, 140–141
Rustichello, 120

Samarkand, 69, 98
Shah Rukh (Persian khan), 125
Shang, city of, 5
Shang Dynasty (1523–1028 B.C.), 5–7, 101
Shang K'o-hsi (Ming general), 147
Shang-tu (Xanadu), 115–116
Shanhaikuan, 33–34, 43, 101, 125, 131, 145, 148–150, 154, 161
Shanking, 101
Shansi, 111, 154
Shantung, 30
Shan-t'o (Turkish tribe), 99
Shen Tsung (Sung emperor), 103
Shen-nung, 4
Shih Huang Ti (Ch'in emperor), 17–29, 33, 35, 37–51, 53–57, 68, 70, 74, 83, 86, 90–91, 128, 137, 156, 158, 162
Shu, kingdom of (founded in 221 A.D.), 83
Shun (Hsia emperor), 4
Silk Road, Old 67–70, 81, 87, 125, 152
Sogdiana, 69
South China Sea, 81, 105
Sowerby, A. de C., 162
Spathary, 153
Ssu of Pao, *see* Pao Ssu
Ssu-ma Ch'ien (historian), 16, 18, 29, 45, 51, 55
Stein, Mark Aurel, 70–72, 81, 97, 159, 163–164
Su Tsung (T'ang emperor), 98

Suchow, 141–142, 154, 163
Sui Dynasty (589–618 A.D.), 90–94
Sun Ts'e (Han warlord), 82
Sung, state of, 10, 16
Sung Dynasty (960–1127 A.D.), 100, 102–104
Sung Dynasty, Southern (1127–1279 A.D.), 105, 108, 112–115, 117
Syria, 80
Szechuan, 83

Ta Shun Dynasty (founded 1644 A.D.), 148
Tai Fu-ku (poet), 106
T'ai Tsung (T'ang emperor, also known as Li Shih-min), 93–96
Taiping, city of, 129
T'ang Dynasty (618–906 A.D.), 94–99, 122, 154, 158, 165
Tangut (tribe), 102–103
Tapai Ho (Big White River), 35
Tashkent, 98
Ta-t'ung, city of, 127
Temujin, *see* Genghis Khan
Three August Ones, 4
Three Kingdoms, 82–84
Ti (tribe), 16
Tibet, 14, 27, 33, 35, 69, 115–116, 154
Tientsin, 155
Time of the Warring States, 9, 83
Timur Khan (Mongol Great Khan and Yuan emperor), 121
T'o-pa (tribe), 84–88, 100, 165
T'o-pa Ssu (T'o-pa Wei emperor), 86
T'o-pa Tao (T'o-pa Wei emperor), 86–87, 151
Ts'ao Ts'ao (Han warlord), 82
T'u-chueh (Turkish tribe), 89–90, 93
T'u-man (Hsiung-nu chieftain), 57–58
Tung-hu (tribe, also known as Hu), 26–27, 56, 58
Tun-huang, 68–69, 71–72, 87, 97, 100, 163
Turkestan, 27
Tzuchingkuan, city of, 111

Tzu-ch'u (king of Ch'in), 18
Tzu-ying (third emperor of Ch'in), 55–56

Uighurs (Turkish tribe), 93, 98–99, 109

Wall of Gog and Magog, 122
Wan-li (Ming emperor), 134–136, 143, 146
Wang (Han empress), 77
Wang Mang (Hsin emperor), 77–79
Warwick, Adam, 161–163
Wei, kingdom of (founded 220 A.D.), 83
Wei, state of, 6, 15, 17, 20, 28
Wei Dynasty, T'o-pa (385–534 A.D.), 85–88
Wen Ti (Han emperor), 60–61
Willow Palisade, 145
Wu (T'ang empress), 96
Wu, kingdom of (222–280 A.D.), 83
Wu, state of, 11, 15
Wu Ling (Chao king), 15
Wu San-kuei (Ming general), 146, 149–152
Wu Ti (Chin emperor), 83–84

Wu Ti (Han emperor), 61, 63–75, 77, 79–80, 83, 90

Yang Chien (Sui emperor), 90
Yang Ti (Sui emperor), 91–95
Yangchow, city of, 91, 116
Yangtze River, 6, 50, 83, 91–92, 104, 108
Yao (Hsia emperor), 4
Yarkand, 116, 140
Yeh-lu Ch'u-ts'ai (Khitan diplomat), 112–113
Yellow River, 2–6, 15, 27, 32–33, 37, 50, 58, 65, 76, 92, 109, 128, 135
Yellow Sea, 5–6, 33, 114
Yen, state of, 6, 10, 15, 17 20, 26
Yenching, see Peking
Yenmen, city of, 131
Ying Tsung (Ming emperor), 127–128
Yu (Hsia emperor), 4
Yu Wang (Chou king), 8–9
Yuan Dynasty (1279–1368 A.D.), 114
Yuan Ti (Han emperor), 75–77
Yueh, state of, 11, 16
Yueh-chih (tribe), 27, 58, 65–66
Yung-lo (Ming emperor, also known as Chu Ti), 123–127

Robert Silverberg specializes in the literary exploration of ancient worlds. His prize-winning *Lost Cities and Vanished Civilizations* took thousands of readers to Thebes, Carthage, Pompeii, Troy, Babylon, Machu Picchu, and Knossos. His *Sunken History: The Story of Underwater Archaeology* was a Junior Literary Guild Selection. In *Empires in the Dust,* he brought to life such ancient civilizations as the Phoenicians, the Etruscans, the Incas, and the dwellers of the Indus Valley. In *Akhnaten, The Rebel Pharaoh,* he recreated the life and times of the first temporal ruler ever to lead his people toward the worship of a single God.